RASPUTIN

*The role of Britain's secret service
in his torture and murder*

RASPUTIN

*The role of Britain's secret service
in his torture and murder*

RICHARD CULLEN

dialogue< >

First published in Great Britain in 2010 by
Dialogue, an imprint of
Biteback Publishing Ltd
Heal House
375 Kennington Lane
London
SE11 5QY

ISBN 978-1-906447-07-6

10 9 8 7 6 5 4 3 2 1

A CIP catalogue record for this book is available from the British Library.

Set in Baskerville by SoapBox

Printed and bound in Great Britain by TJ International Ltd, Padstow, Cornwall

CONTENTS

This book is dedicated to
the eternal memory of:

Sergeant Simon Valentine
Corporal Joseph Etchells
Lance Corporal James Fullerton
Fusiliers Petero Suesue, Simon Annis, Louis Carter and Shaun Bush

2nd Battalion, Royal Regiment of Fusiliers,
who were killed while serving their Queen and country
in Helmand Province, Afghanistan in 2009

'And upon this charge; cry God for Harry,
England and St George.'
Shakespeare, *Henry V*

The author is proud to support the charity Help for Heroes
and all his royalties from this book will be donated to the charity

ACKNOWLEDGEMENTS

To the BBC, Lion TV and the Discovery Channel for giving me the opportunity to forensically reinvestigate the evidence and circumstances surrounding Rasputin's murder for their documentary 'Who Killed Rasputin?'.

To my close friend, the internationally esteemed academic Viktor Petrovich Salnikov, the former rector of St Petersburg Ministry of Interior Affairs (MVD) University, and to all my friends and colleagues at the university who have on so many occasions made me a welcomed guest to Russia, who helped in my research and obtained the permissions from various Russian institutions and individuals to use the material contained in this book.

To Dr Gerald Brooke, who has been and still is my friend and mentor in all things Russian. He was ultimately the catalyst to my being asked to carry out the reinvestigation by the producer/director of 'Who Killed Rasputin?', Mike Wadding.

To Professor Derrick Pounder, head of the Centre for Forensic Medicine at the University of Dundee, for his advice and support during the early stages of this reinvestigation.

To Martin Parker, lead forensic scientist at the National Ballistics Intelligence Service, for his advice, opinion and support.

To Nicholas A. Ohotin, communications director of the Synod of Bishops of the Russian Orthodox Church Outside of Russia.

To Professor Joe Fuhrmann for his insights around the life and death of Rasputin.

To Phil Tomaselli, my friend, whose research skills and knowledge of the period I much admire.

To Greg King, the author of such books as *Fate of the Romanovs*, who kindly acted as my editor, and advised, guided and supported me through the drafting process.

To Rudy De Casseres, who lives in Helsinki, is multilingual and a real expert in all things Rasputin and has given me so much assistance and advice in writing this book.

To Andrew Cook, who acted as the historical consultant to 'Who Killed Rasputin?', discovered the SIS link and wrote the 2005 book *To Kill Rasputin*.

To the many friends I have made through the Alexander Palace website who have encouraged and helped me understand the Russia of 1916. In particular I have to thank Rob Monash and Bob Atchison, who together with Brian Jones have raised many issues regarding the murder, the parties involved and the Yusupov Palace. Access to and the use in this book of their online resources has been invaluable.

To my publishers, Biteback, in particular Michael Smith for his encouragement and support and Jonathan Wadman for his patience in editing this book and in particular for his Russian language skills, which were especially evident during the editing process.

Lastly and most importantly to my wife Christine and our three daughters, Charlotte, Felicity and Nicola, without whose love, patience, humour, support and understanding this book could not have been written.

PREFACE

The amount of new evidence that we uncovered during our reinvestigation of Grigorii Rasputin's death for the BBC programme 'Who Killed Rasputin?', part of the *Timewatch* strand, would have allowed it to be a three-programme series in its own right. In this book I have tried to encapsulate all that we disclosed in the programme and build around it the plethora of other relevant facts and intelligence I have since discovered. I initially concentrated on the forensic reinvestigation of the murder but moved on to probe the issue of British involvement in it. I have concentrated on the evidence I discovered before, during and after the production. I am firmly convinced that Rasputin was killed as the result of a plot hatched by the British Secret Intelligence Service and that Oswald Rayner, a close friend of Feliks Yusupov, fired the fatal shot.

I became involved in the programme early in 2004, when Mike Wadding asked me to reflect on how Rasputin died. I started by rereading Edvard Radzinskii's *Rasputin: The Last Word*,[1] and by the end of that day I wondered whether I had ever really read it before, as forensic facts and evidence I had previously glossed over grew in importance. Reading the accounts of the murder by Yusupov and Vladimir Purishkevich, a member of the Duma, made me realise that their stories were substantially composed of untruths. For so many years, like so many others, I had missed the truths of Rasputin's death. I applied my knowledge and skills learned over the years as a detective and a keen student of forensic medicine.

For the last five years books relating to Rasputin have been my constant companion; as I said to my friend Phil Tomaselli, 'I live the case every day'. My thoughts have moved on considerably since the *Timewatch* programme, partly because I have revisited the forensics yet again and partly because I had missed things in my past assessments of the evidence.

This book is for those who have an interest in Rasputin's death and in particular the forensic aspects of his murder. For our purposes 'forensic' means 'of the court' and therefore encompasses all evidence that could be placed before a criminal court. It is not intended to be a glossy semi-historical novel but an exciting, evidential trip through the murder of Rasputin – enjoy it as such. It is based on fact and not fiction.

I joined the Metropolitan Police Service in 1971 and rose to the rank of commander, the equivalent to assistant chief constable in a British provincial police force. In that role I headed Europe's largest police training and development school, the Peel Centre, Hendon. From almost my first day in post in August 1997, I became involved in a programme funded by the British government's Department for International Development that was targeted at the development of officer cadets from the Russian Ministry of Interior's police training academies, in particular St Petersburg MVD University, a relationship which continues to this day. I have lectured many groups of Russian police officers, both senior and junior.

I retired from the Met in September 2001 and began to study Russian history, with a particular focus on the reign of Tsar Nicholas II. Any research into this period must include a study of the 'dark forces' of Grigorii Rasputin.

My starting point for this reinvestigation was not the possible involvement of the British but the deconstruction and then reconstruction of the evidence of the alleged witnesses to the murder and the available forensic intelligence. This analysis blows apart the previously accepted theories relating to Rasputin's death.

I am grateful for the comments of Greg King and Penny Wilson in their book *The Fate of the Romanovs*,[2] where they discuss the criticism that new theories attract when applied to well-established historical belief, be that perceived knowledge, fact or fiction. In this book I am challenging the historical beliefs of many and, as King and Wilson say, this is more complicated when there are romantic, religious and political sentiments involved. By deconstructing the evidence of the known witnesses to the plot to kill and the actual murder of Rasputin, together with a detailed forensic analysis, I am overturning many dearly held sentimental theories of how he met his end. For many the fact that this was not some heroic battle by Yusupov and his friends to save the Holy Russian Empire and the Romanov dynasty, but was rather a shoddy and cowardly murder, will be both unbearable and unacceptable. The facts as related by Yusupov in his memoirs and Purishkevich, together with the only other short account we have from any of the other alleged conspirators, that of Dr Stanislaus de Lazovert, are a substantial series of lies designed to pervert the course of justice and hide the identity of the real killer or killers.

I make no apology to those who are steeped in knowledge of Rasputin and his demise. I present this reinvestigation as if I was investigating it now, absorbing all the evidence, primary and secondary, direct and hearsay. My purpose has always been to discover the truth and, behind that, the involvement of the Secret Intelligence Service in the plot to assassinate Rasputin.

I have referenced the various books and documents that I refer to in the text by way of endnotes. I have attributed all material that is not mine.

I refer to some aspects of the lives of the victim, the conspirators, the Tsar and Tsaritsa and others associated with the victim. However, it is not my intention to delve deeply into their histories except where it is relevant to the plot to kill Rasputin and its possible motives. You can find out much about those mentioned and life under the Romanovs in general by visiting the Alexander Palace Russian history website, www.alexanderpalace.org.

INTRODUCTION

This is not a prequel to the *Lord of the Rings* trilogy, yet it is a tale of which even Tolkien would have been rightly proud. A story in which the forces of good, 'the Fellowship', are pitted against the pervasive, evil and almost immortal 'dark forces' abroad in their land. This fantastic tale, as told by two of the Fellowship, has for over ninety years been the accepted and largely unchallenged version of the events surrounding Grigorii Rasputin's death in 1916.

The setting is a vast kingdom ruled by an inadequate and ill-prepared autocratic emperor who, with his manipulative, probably megalomaniac, foreign wife, believed in the divine right of kings. The couple struggled to produce a male heir to the throne, parenting four daughters until the birth of their youngest child, a haemophiliac son, in a country whose manhood was being bled dry in the third year of the 'war to end wars'. The war was not going well for the emperor or his people. There was talk of revolution, of sedition, of the end of a dynasty. The forces of evil were everywhere to be seen.

The Fellowship was headed by the hero of the tale, a foppish, charismatic, attractive, foreign-university-educated, bisexual (probably homosexual), cross-dressing socialite who was the much-travelled surviving male heir to the largest fortune in the country. His family could trace its heritage back to Aboubekir ben Raioc, who lived in the sixth century and who was said to be a descendant of the Prophet Ali. He was the supreme head of Muslims and bore the titles Emir el Mora, Prince of Princes, Sultan of Sultans and Khan.

He was joined by four others: his close friend, a grand duke, who was the favoured cousin of the emperor; an extrovert, larger-than-life monarchist who was a member of the country's parliament and who ran, at his own expense, a hospital train that brought injured soldiers back from the front; a doctor of medicine who had displayed bravery in front of enemy guns to treat and rescue injured soldiers; and a soldier, a close and trusted friend who would in 1921 marry Tolstoy's granddaughter.

Their purpose was to rid the country of the 'dark forces' that they believed held undue sway over the emperor and empress in matters of state and the prosecution of the war, all of which they and others in the aristocracy were convinced would ultimately lead to the collapse of the dynasty and the established order.

These dark forces were embodied in a self-professed 'holy man' – indeed, the phrase became his sobriquet. He held a pernicious and malign influence over the Emperor and Empress, but particularly over the Empress. His mysticism, hypnotism and alleged powers of healing had won him her devotion, as he appeared to be the only person able to help the heir to the throne as he battled with haemophilia. He was an increasingly drunken serial debaucher, who was as happy in the company of prostitutes and gypsies as he was with the aristocracy and the royal family. He allegedly predicted that his demise would be followed closely by the collapse of the dynasty.

The Fellowship enticed 'Dark Forces' to a clandestine engagement in the basement of the hero's parents' house. They attempted to poison him using potassium cyanide grated into cakes and glasses of wine. When he proved resistant to the poison our hero shot him once at close quarters, the bullet passing through the stomach and liver. To all appearances he was dead, yet some time later he miraculously recovered, wrestled with the hero and then ran upstairs to escape into a snow-covered courtyard.

The member of parliament drew his pistol, chased after Dark Forces and fired twice from about 20 yards, hitting him in the back. One bullet passed through a kidney and the other the back of the head. The gunman walked over to where Dark Forces lay and kicked him in the temple. Helpers took the apparently lifeless body into the house, where our hero viciously assaulted it using a brass door handle encased in rubber. Eventually it was wrapped in 'blue material' and driven to a bridge where there was a gap in the thick winter ice that covered the river. The body was thrown in, but Dark Forces was still alive and fought to free his bonds until eventually succumbing to the frozen waters of the river.

Unfortunately there is not a *Lord of the Rings: The Return of the King* outcome to this story. Dark Forces' demise did not lift the spectre of evil from the land; instead a new and enduring evil descended with an all-pervading darkness: revolution burst forth, the old order crumbled and the years of Bolshevism, communism, terror and repression arrived. As Dark Forces allegedly prophesied:

I write and leave behind me this letter at St Petersburg. I feel that I shall leave life before 1 January. I wish to make known to the Russian people, to Papa, to the Russian Mother and to the children, to the land of Russia, what they must understand. If common assassins kill me, and especially my brothers the Russian peasants, you, Tsar of Russia, have nothing to fear: remain on your throne and govern, and you, Russian Tsar, will have nothing to fear for your children; they will reign for hundreds of years in Russia. But if I am murdered by boyars and nobles, if they shed my blood, their hands will remain soiled with my blood; for twenty-five years they will not wash their hands from my blood. They will leave Russia. Brother will kill brother, and they will kill each other and hate each other, and for twenty-five years there will be no nobility in the country. Tsar of the land of Russia, if you hear the sound of the bell which will tell you that Grigorii has been killed, you must know this: if it was your relations who wrought my death then no one of your family, that is to say, none of your children or relations, will remain alive for more than two years. They will be killed by the Russian people . . . I shall be killed. I am no longer among the living. Pray, pray, be strong, think of your blessed family.

Twenty-three days after this letter was allegedly dated, on 17 December,* Rasputin was murdered.

On 17 July 1918 (Gregorian calendar), Tsar Nicholas II, his wife Empress Alexandra, their five children, their doctor and three attendants were herded into the cellar of 'the house of special purpose' (the Ipat'yev house) in Yekaterinburg. Nicholas had been forced to abdicate a year earlier as civil war gripped the country. He and his family were forced into exile in this Ural mountains city. Their Bolshevik captors raised their guns and proceeded to slaughter the imperial family and their attendants. Some of the bullets were deflected by the jewels sewn into the women's dresses. The firing squad used bayonets to finish them off.

The bodies were dumped into a mine shaft. They were later retrieved as word of the killings spread. The death squad tried burning two of the bodies – but it took too long. They doused the

---

* In 1916 Russia still used the Julian calendar, whose dates were then thirteen days behind those of the Gregorian calendar. Except where specified, I have used the Julian dating system for the purposes of this book. Just to highlight this, Rasputin was murdered in the early hours of 17 December in the Julian calendar, which would translate into 30 December in the Gregorian calendar.

rest of them with sulphuric acid and buried them in a shallow grave in a forest outside the city.

It has been suggested that the above quote, which appeared after the regicide of the imperial family, was written by Aron Simanovich, Rasputin's secretary, and as such is a forgery. What cannot be doubted is that Rasputin on numerous recorded occasions predicted the downfall of the monarchy if he should meet an untimely death.

Few characters in history have been the subject of so many books, articles, films and television documentaries as Rasputin. Boney M.'s song 'Rasputin', with its chorus 'Ra-Ra-Rasputin, lover of the Russian Queen', and a starring role in the Fox cartoon *Anastasia* are just two products of the interest surrounding this unique man's life and death.

The story of the plot to kill Rasputin and the murder itself reads like fiction, and as far back as 1917 that is how Maurice Paléologue, the French ambassador to Nicholas's court, described it in his diary, which was published as part of his memoirs in 1925:

> Prince Feliks Yusupov is twenty-nine and gifted with quick wits and aesthetic tastes; but his dilettantism is rather too prone to perverse imaginings and literary representations of vice and death. So I am afraid that he has regarded the murder of Rasputin mainly as a scenario worthy of his favourite author, Oscar Wilde. In any case his instincts, countenance and manner make him much closer akin to the hero of *Dorian Grey* than to Brutus or Lorenzaccio.[1]

Determining what is fact, what is fiction, what is myth and what is real is difficult when researching and studying Rasputin. The saint–devil continuum is ever present and, depending on which biography or history you read, there will be a different perspective on this unique man's life and death. Some were sad, in fact grief stricken by his demise, but others were ecstatic and overjoyed that he was dead. William Le Queux, quoting a manuscript prepared by one of Rasputin's former members of staff, says: 'Next night, however, a thrill went through the Court, as well as through the Russian people, by the six-word announcement in the Exchange Newspapers, which coldly said: "Gregory Rasputin has ceased to exist."'[2]

When Mike Wadding approached me to reinvestigate the 1916 murder of Rasputin for *Timewatch*, I was provided with a minimum of information; at this time there was no hint of any British involvement. All that I could base my initial research on was the previous published account of the murder and more recent books regarding his death.

I spent hours painstakingly comparing the two alleged murderers' published versions of his demise and established numerous and significant discrepancies in what they said. I had to doubt whether they had been present at the same event or whether either of them had been present at all. Next I worked through the forensics and quickly dismantled the existing myths around his death. I found he was not poisoned, he did not drown and he was shot three times at close range, none of which fitted with the existing stories.

Gradually I was fed more information, including the 1993 assessment of the original post mortem by Professor Vladimir Zharov, head of the Forensic Medical Analysis Bureau and as such Russia's leading pathologist, together with two other esteemed pathologists. I then received the files from the Russian State Archive (GARF) about his death, including witness statements, and finally, while filming in St Petersburg, gained access to the original scene-of-crime photographs. I was given some information about British involvement and, just as I was about to do a piece to camera in the Astoria Hotel, was shown a letter from a SIS officer that implied British involvement in the murder.

But the *Timewatch* programme, as good as it was, was out of context and skimmed the surface of the murder, sticking too much to the old romanticised story. I was already beginning to realise from my research that the fondly held, accepted and romantic, heroic versions of the murder were fabricated nonsense, a tangled web of lies, intended to deceive. My search for the truth did not end with the programme; I needed to do more research in London and St Petersburg, revisit the scene and the forensic evidence, look at timelines, map locations and the positions of individuals at critical moments, and consider in detail the British involvement. I talked and worked with my friends at the Ministry of Interior Affairs (MVD) University in St Petersburg in the search for the truth, in short to carry out a full and proper investigation of all the evidence. Much of this evidence had remained hidden for nearly a century.

It is my objective view, based on the evidence available, that the accepted version of events concerning the murder of Rasputin was the culmination of a major conspiracy to pervert the course of justice and was designed to conceal the true identity of the conspirators and certainly his murderers.

I have investigated many murders, some of which have involved extreme physical violence and some both torture and shooting. I have often watched on television or read in the media as senior detectives describe a murder as 'the most brutal I have ever seen' or the 'most sadistic I have ever seen'. I investigated the torture and shooting of a drug-dealing father and son in which the injuries were horrible, but their murder was nowhere near as brutal as that of Rasputin. There was nothing heroic or romantic in Rasputin's demise; it was violent, brutal and depraved, and he must, I believe, have suffered considerably before a shot to his forehead put an end to his suffering. This book describes what my investigation found.

This is the truth about the brutal torture and murder of Grigorii Yefimovich Rasputin.

The city, the river, the climate – the ice

To help the reader it might be useful to understand a little of St Petersburg. The northernmost major city of the world, it is built on a series of islands linked by bridges. I am in awe of St Petersburg; I love its history, its ambience, its gaiety and the warmth of its people.

Due to the city's northern position it enjoys the phenomenon of the 'white nights', lasting from 25/26 May till 16/17 July. The longest day has 18 hours 53 minutes of daylight. The shortest day is 22 December (5 hours 52 minutes of daylight). The importance of the time span of the shortest day and its relevance to the investigation will become obvious.

The river Neva is the city's main waterway. The name of the river derives from 'Nevo', the ancient name of Lake Ladoga, which is its source. The river runs into the Gulf of Finland and is 74 kilometres long, flowing for 32 kilometres within the city boundaries. The average width of the Neva within the city is 600 metres and the maximum depth 24 metres. In the delta, it splits into three main branches: the Bol'shaya Neva, the Malaya Nevka and the Bol'shaya Nevka.

The average winter temperature is minus 8 degrees Celsius. The temperature frequently drops to lows of minus 25 or minus 30 degrees in the winter. The Neva and its branches normally become frozen over between 25 November and 5 December and the ice is gone by mid-April. I first visited St Petersburg at the end of November 1997; by the time I left on 5 December the Neva was frozen solid to some considerable depth with large ice floes rising out of it.

Chapter One

THE MAIN PLAYERS

Rasputin – an overview of a victim

Before detailing Rasputin's life I feel a need to say where I stand on the saint–devil continuum that has been debated over the years in relation to our murder victim. The *New Oxford Dictionary of English* definition of evil is: 'Profound immorality, wickedness, and depravity, especially when regarded as a supernatural force.' On that basis, excluding the supernatural bit, Rasputin was evil. However, to many of the Russian imperial family, nobility and politicians he was considered to possess supernatural powers – he was, as we have seen and shall see again, dubbed with the title 'Dark Forces'.

My understanding of an evil person is someone who does harm to others. I view Hitler, Stalin and Pol Pot as evil. Rasputin was debauched, he was profoundly immoral, he was manipulative, arrogant, repulsive, depraved and to some extent wicked, yet what physical harm did he do to others? Some say he caused the 1917 revolution and the downfall of the Romanov dynasty. I would recommend that such people read Russian history and the insights that are obtained from authors such as Orlando Figes in *A People's Tragedy*.[1]

In my mind, despite the fact that I have a dislike for what he stood for and his behaviour, the informal power he exerted, although in a depraved way, has parallels in this country with Reginald, 2nd Viscount Esher (Lord Esher), who held informal power over the reigns of three monarchs – Victoria, Edward VII and George V. Maybe he was a version of an early 'spin doctor' but it is my belief that he has been harshly treated. Another person, in another time, with fewer perversions might have been hailed a hero, the barely literate peasant who became the imperial family's advisor in chief.

Grigorii Yefimovich Rasputin was a peasant (*muzhik*), born in the Siberian town of Pokrovskoe on 10 January 1869. During his childhood and as a young man he could best be described as a yob. Some biographers and historians say he was violent, frequently drunk and a petty thief. Rasputin allegedly underwent a religious transformation around the age of eighteen and spent three months in the Verkhotur'ye monastery. When he returned to Pokrovskoe he was a changed man. Though he married Praskov'ya Fyodorovna and had three children with her (two girls and a boy), he began to wander as a *strannik* or pilgrim. During his journeyings, Rasputin travelled to Greece and Jerusalem. Though he often returned to Pokrovskoe, he found himself in St Petersburg in 1903. By then he was proclaimed by some as a *starets*, an elder, who had healing powers and could predict the future.

It is interesting to note that Rasputin was frequently linked to a religious sect called the Khlysty, a group of debauched flagellants that were said to indulge in group sex. This Christian sect that combined both paganism and Orthodoxy found a home in backward Russia. Rasputin was investigated on a number of occasions with regard to his membership of the sect, but there is no proof that he did indulge in Khlysty rituals.

He managed to dupe many Orthodox Church leaders, some for ever, but others eventually realised what he really was and were to become some of his most outspoken opponents. One of these, the monk Iliodor, later emigrated to America and, using his given name of Sergei Trufanov, was the most vocal antagonist of his ex-supporters.

Rasputin began to move in powerful circles, the mysticism and spiritualism surrounding him attracting a growing band of influential women. He first met the Tsar on 1 November 1905. It was thus that he felt able to write to him, offering to bring him a powerful icon.

He was first invited to the royal palace in October 1906, bringing the icon with him. Subsequently he displayed what the royal couple thought to be healing powers. Unlike his predecessors, Rasputin appeared able to help the haemophilic heir to the throne. How did he do it? That is still greatly disputed. Some people believe Rasputin used hypnotism; others say he didn't know how to hypnotise. Part of Rasputin's continued mystique is the remaining question as to whether he really had the powers he claimed to have. Medical science tends to suggest that the type of bleeding that Aleksei suffered from stops of its own accord, so Rasputin may have just been in the right place, at the right time.

Having proven to Alexandra his alleged holy powers, Rasputin did not remain just the healer for Aleksei; he became Alexandra's confidant and personal advisor sometime after 1912. To the aristocrats, having a peasant advising the Tsaritsa, who in turn held a great deal of influence over the Tsar, was unacceptable. In addition, Rasputin was a lover of alcohol and sex – both of which he consumed in excess.

Though Rasputin appeared a pious and saintly holy man in front of the royal couple, others saw him as a dirty, drunken, sex-craved peasant who was ruining Russia and the monarchy. It didn't help that Rasputin was portrayed as having sex with women in high society in exchange for granting political favours. Nor that many in Russia believed, incorrectly, that Rasputin and the Tsaritsa were lovers and wanted to make a separate peace with the Germans (Russia and Germany were enemies during the First World War).

So dependent was Alexandra on Rasputin, who she described in letters to Nicholas as 'Our Friend', that his advice was taken on many issues and he manipulated the promotion to high rank of politicians and church leaders alike. Nicholas gave in to her incessant droning and nagging. Those who stood or spoke against him tended to fall from royal grace.

For much of the time from when he first met the royal family until his death on 17 December 1916 Rasputin was under almost constant surveillance by one arm of the police or another.

His alleged murderers – the accepted version

Prince Feliks Feliksovich Yusupov (1887–1967)

Feliks Yusupov's life is fully set out in his autobiography, *Lost Splendour*.[2] He was born on 24 March 1887 and at the time of Rasputin's death was twenty-nine years old. He was the sole surviving male heir to the Yusupov family's fortune. His elder brother by five years, Nikolai, had been killed in a duel some years previously.

The Yusupov family was allegedly the wealthiest in Russia and in addition to the Yusupov Palace on the river Moika in St Petersburg, where Rasputin was to die, they had numerous other palaces scattered across Russia and the Crimea. A direct descendant of Yusuf Khan, on conversion to the Orthodox faith Abdul Mirza took the name of Dmitrii and the title of Prince Yusupov from Tsar Theodore. Over the years the Yusupov family acquired its wealth until its fortunes were greater than those of the Tsar. Close to the royal family, the Yusupovs' relationships with them were to deteriorate due to Rasputin's malign influence.

It is hard to see what Feliks Yusupov did with his life, although he travelled extensively and in 1909 went to University College, Oxford, where he was to meet his lifelong friend Oswald Rayner, who was at Oriel College. He didn't join the Army in 1914, because Russian law allowed a lone son not to go to war. However, he did join the Corps des Pages, a sort of Territorial Army at best. Also in 1914 he married Irina, the niece of the Tsar, and they remained together until his death in 1967. They pursued to conclusion successful libel suits in respect of films and publications about Rasputin.

After the revolution Yusupov spent most of his life as an émigré in Paris. He first published his memoirs of the murder in 1927 and a number of later versions have emerged, all with their unique differences.

Dmitrii Pavlovich Romanov, Grand Duke of Russia (1891–1942)

I intend to cover the life of Dmitrii in some detail, as he is an intriguing character and he never published his account of Rasputin's murder. I have used Lisa Davidson's biography of him as the basis of this biographical detail.[3] He swore to his father on the Holy Cross that he did not murder Rasputin. He never spoke to Yusupov during their long exile because of his former friend's loose tongue about the conspiracy to kill Rasputin.

Dmitrii was the only son of Princess Alexandra of Greece and Grand Duke Pavel Aleksandrovich. He was born in 1891 and at the time of Rasputin's murder was twenty-five years old. The beginning of Dmitrii's unstable childhood can be traced to the death of his mother in childbirth. He was afforded the material splendour of a Russian grand duke and the emotional poverty of a motherless child. His widower father, brother of Alexander III and uncle to Nicholas II, became entangled in the matrimonial scandals that plagued the

5

later Romanovs. Dmitrii and his older sister, Mariya Pavlovna, then became part of the household of his aunt and uncle, Grand Duke Sergei Aleksandrovich and Grand Duchess Elisabeth. These two were an interesting couple: Sergei was the sadistic, anti-Semitic governor general of Moscow, while Elisabeth, or Ella, later became a nun. Ella and Sergei had no children of their own. Because no one else was available to him, and because she was a loving person, Dmitrii got whatever nurturing he could from Grand Duchess Ella. The chief difficulty of any child who has known this type of upheaval is in the forming of attachments with others, but Dmitrii and Ella were to remain close throughout her life.

The kindly Grand Duke Pavel was often absent during his son's childhood, due to the matrimonial difficulties mentioned above. He greatly distressed his family when, in 1902, he married a commoner and a divorcee, Ol'ga von Pistohlkors, with whom he had three children. For a time, Pavel Aleksandrovich was exiled to Paris, returning to his home in Tsarskoe Selo during World War I, at the command of the Tsar. His wife was eventually granted the courtesy title Princess Palei and died in 1929.

In a sense, Dmitrii was orphaned twice over, due to Pavel's absence and the unlikely possibility that Sergei had any paternal influence over the young Dmitrii. It is uncertain if this vacuum was ever filled. If it was, the only possibility was his first cousin, Nicholas II. While their fathers were brothers, the Tsar was twenty-three years his senior. We can only speculate that, because he often lived in the Alexander Palace and other imperial residences with Nicholas and his family, Dmitrii may have been like a son to the last Tsar.

In 1905, Sergei became victim to a bomb thrown by revolutionary terrorists led by Boris Savinkov, continuing the line of premature deaths of those associated with Dmitrii that began with his mother.

It was at this point that Ella became a nun, founding a convent in Moscow. She lived in relative obscurity, and makes appearances on the historic canvas only twice more.

In 1916, Ella appealed to her sister, the Tsaritsa, to send Rasputin away. They parted, for the last time, acrimoniously. In July 1918, one day after the murder of the imperial family, the nun was thrown alive down a mineshaft in Siberia. Her body was discovered by the Whites in the Civil War and transported to Jerusalem, where she was buried.

Nicholas and Alexandra were very fond of young Dmitrii. In fact, some evidence exists that they wanted him to marry their eldest daughter, Ol'ga, and pass on the throne to them jointly, in the likely event Aleksei did not survive childhood. Nicholas's willingness to tamper with the order of succession is well documented. In fact, his 1917 abdication on behalf of Aleksei was illegal under existing law. The impediment to implementing this alternative succession plan was not Dmitrii, but Ol'ga. We know she was serious and very religious. By then, Dmitrii had grown up, but not matured. While Ol'ga and her sisters are frequently characterised as immature, her refusal in this matter of succession could be evidence to the contrary. Dmitrii's love of high living and comparatively loose ways very likely shocked the more strait-laced Ol'ga.

Dmitrii and Ol'ga were first cousins once removed, a connection she may have felt was not healthy for any children they would have together. As the daughter of two individuals deeply in love, she may have wished for the same for her marriage. But regardless of her reasoning, we do know that Ol'ga was steadfast in her refusal to enter into a dynastic marriage. This did not estrange Dmitrii from his imperial cousins. He continued to flirt with the other grand duchesses and enjoyed a high degree of intimacy with the family. Alexandra, in her diaries, despaired of his involvement with a fast social set. All of this indicates a great closeness, at least on the part of Nicholas and Alexandra. With his likely difficulties in forming attachments, what were his feelings towards them in 1916?

There are many unanswered questions regarding Dmitrii's involvement in the plot to kill Rasputin. If Rasputin's role in the family was merely as a healer or spiritual advisor, it would be unlikely that Dmitrii, or any of the others associated with the plot, would have sought to kill him. If Dmitrii was the carefree person he appeared in public, we must ask ourselves: why did he become involved in a murder plot?

But involved it seems he was. The conspirators were shielded from the law, as grand dukes were answerable only to the Tsar for their actions. Dmitrii, then, reveals himself as more purposeful than his image. But what was his purpose? History shows that Rasputin had ventured outside the narrow confines that would have made his association with the imperial couple acceptable. He sought, and obtained, political influence, at least with Alexandra. There are two theories, both compelling, which could explain Dmitrii's motives. The one put forth by Yusupov is that Rasputin was murdered out of Russian patriotism. They thought that, with Rasputin dead, the Tsar could reclaim his slipping prestige. While it seems foolish in hindsight, this motive is possible in respect of Dmitrii.

His cousin, the Tsar, was away commanding his army, and his wife and children were being smeared almost daily in the tabloids with lurid, if untrue, stories involving Rasputin. Dmitrii knew Nicholas well enough to know that he would not listen to the family's advice. He remained close to Ella, an outspoken critic of Rasputin. His cousin's reputation was suffering, and the only mother he had ever known was urging Rasputin's removal but being rebuffed by her sister, Alexandra; would that have been sufficient motive for Dmitrii?

The other theory, never published but divulged by Mariya Pavlovna after her brother's death, was that Rasputin was preparing to go to the Tsaritsa with damaging information about the flamboyant Prince Yusupov. We know that the imperial family were concerned about Dmitrii's relationship with Yusupov and the weight of opinion falls heavily on the side that they were lovers of some kind. The patriotic motive, Mariya told friends, was a cover for the true reason, and was concocted after the fact. The 'dead men tell no tales' theory does have a certain appeal. However, there are several problems with it.

This theory presumes a high degree of loyalty on Dmitrii's part to Feliks Yusupov. It has already been established that the type of attachment this would involve would have been difficult, if not impossible, for Dmitrii as a young adult. The two did not in fact remain friends in exile, although only after Feliks had failed to keep his mouth shut about the murder. Second, the third conspirator was a member of the Duma. Vladimir Purishkevich had no known connection to the other two except for his desire to remove Rasputin. Feliks and Dmitrii may have brought Purishkevich into the plot to raise the banner of patriotism and as someone who had no connection to the various alleged sexual intrigues.

The precise political motive may never be known. One may accept what Yusupov wrote as true. But there is a more interesting theory that would fit exactly with what we know about Dmitrii. It is known that he was mentioned as a successor to Nicholas during the revolution of 1905, and also that there were numerous plots in 1916–17 to remove the Tsar by members of the Romanov family. Most frequently mentioned in the later plotting was Grand Duke Nikolai Mikhailovich, former Commander-in-Chief. But he refused to join in a palace revolution. There is some speculation, although the evidence around this is very weak, that Rasputin's murder was the opening act of a plot to remove Nicholas and replace him with Dmitrii. This would, if in the unlikely event of it being true, also explain his participation better than the first theory.

However, this is still speculative. It's not too difficult to imagine the great anger and hurt Nicholas and Alexandra felt upon learning of Dmitrii's betrayal, on whatever level, in December 1916. Not only did they lose Father Grigorii, they also lost Dmitrii. In punishing him, as has been established, they saved his life. They most certainly knew of this irony before they themselves were murdered.

Vladimir Mitrofanovich Purishkevich – deputy in the State Duma (1870–1920)
Biographical details for the three other conspirators in the accepted version of events are somewhat lacking.

Purishkevich came from a wealthy landowning family in Bessarabia. His family's origins were apparently Moldavian, but the family had attained noble status some three generations before his birth. His grandfather had been an archpriest in the Moldavian church, and his father had served as president of the Akkerman District Committee.

Purishkevich entered public life between 1902 and 1904 as a member of a special commission in the Ministry of the Interior. He was a reactionary monarchist and served in the Duma because the Tsar had been forced to establish it and Purishkevich, along with other monarchist members, wished to limit its powers. Thus, his purpose was not to represent society, but to champion autocracy. He was elected to the Second Duma, but it was not until the Third and Fourth Dumas (1907–17) that he was able to develop fully his particular political style. Whenever possible Purishkevich sought to disrupt the Duma's proceedings, to abuse opponents in the moderate and left parties, and even hurl insults at the Duma's president. Nor did he restrict himself to verbal abuse: he would also show his disdain for this representative body by his non-verbal communication, once appearing with a flower protruding from his trouser flies. There is also substantial evidence that Purishkevich was an active member of a number of ultra-reactionary groups, including the Black Hundreds, which financed pogroms against the Jews.

Purishkevich dedicated himself to the war effort. Primarily engaged on the Romanian and southern fronts, he was involved in obtaining medical and other supplies for the army. At the time of Rasputin's murder he was running a hospital train back and forth to the front. He escaped arrest as he left Petrograd on the morning after the murder.*

He became known to Yusupov through his speech in the Duma on 19 November 1916:

Evil comes from those 'dark forces' and influences that have forced the accession to high posts of people incapable to occupy them . . . from the influences that are headed by Grishka Rasputin. I have not been able to sleep the last few nights, I give you my word. I have been lying with my eyes wide open imagining the series of telegrams, notes, and reports that the illiterate peasant has written first to one minister and then to another . . . There have been instances where the non-fulfilment of his demands has resulted in those gentlemen, although strong and powerful, being removed from office. Over the 2½ years of the war I have assumed that our domestic quarrels should be forgotten. Now I have violated that prohibition in order to place at the feet of

---

* The city was called St Petersburg from its foundation in 1703 until 1914, whereupon it was given the less Germanic-sounding name Petrograd. In 1924 it was renamed Leningrad and reverted to its original name in 1991.

the throne the thoughts of the Russian masses and the bitter taste of
resentment from the Russian front that have been produced by the
Tsar's ministers who have been turned into marionettes, marionettes
whose threads have been taken firmly in hand by Rasputin and the
Empress Alexandra Fyodorovna – the evil genius of Russia and the
Tsaritsa who has remained German on the Russian throne and alien
to the country and its people.

Purishkevich published his account of the murder in 1918
under the title *The Purishkevich Diary*; a later edition with a foreword
by Vladimir Maklakov, who Yusupov says provided the potassium
cyanide with which they attempted to poison Rasputin (which
Maklakov denied), was published in 1923, three years after
Purishkevich's death. Maklakov was resident in Paris at the time.

Dr Stanislaus de Lazovert

Of Polish origin, Lazovert was a doctor attached to Purishkevich's
hospital train. Purishkevich describes him as 'an old doctor'. He had
been honoured for his heroism under fire whist rescuing soldiers.
We know little of him; searches of the internet show him popping up
at society events after Rasputin's murder and the 1917 revolution.
Purishkevich suggests that he was recruited to act as chauffeur of
the vehicle that was to collect Rasputin on that fateful night. He
also allegedly grated the potassium cyanide into the petits fours. It
will be seen later that one of the suggestions, even if one accepts the
hypothesis that Rasputin was fed cyanide, was that Lazovert might
have been unaware that the cyanide had 'gone off' and was no longer
potent. A rather major failing for an experienced doctor! If you accept
the point that cyanide was administered, would Lazovert have been
unaware of the poison's smell? Professor Vladimir Zharov, in his

reassessment of Rasputin's post mortem, comments that Professor Dmitrii Kosorotov, the initial pathologist, failed to identify the smell of almonds.

Lieutenant Sergei Mikhailovich Sukhotin (1887–1926)
If we know little about Lazovert we know even less about Sukhotin. Greg King, Brian Moynahan and Joe Fuhrmann state that he was Ivan Sukhotin, an officer in the Preobrazhenskii Regiment. Edvard Radzinskii, Feliks Yusupov and others just use the surname, but Rudy De Casseres had established that his first name was Sergei. On page 15 of the 2 April 1932 issue of the Paris-published Russian magazine *Illyustrirovannaya Rossiya* ('Russia Illustrated'), A. Gulevich, chairman of the Union of Preobrazhenskii, wrote: 'In order to maintain the historical truth I have the honour to inform you that no Officer Sukhotin has served in the Life Guards' Preobrazhenskii Regiment.' We know that Sukhotin's brother was trusted by Yusupov and his mother as he used to convey letters between the two: 'I am expecting Sukhotin, in the hope of getting your letter at last,' wrote Princess Zinaida Yusupova to Feliks on 11 December 1916. Sukhotin married Tolstoy's granddaughter Sof'ya Andreevna Tolstaya in 1921. He died in Paris in 1926, his wife in 1957.

What has changed

Edvard Radzinskii boldly subtitled his book on Rasputin published in 2000 'The Last Word'; my analysis of the facts shows that his conclusions about Rasputin's death are far from the 'last word' and I believe that there is still much to be said.

While the memoirs of Feliks Yusupov, most recently resurfacing in a reprint titled *Lost Splendour*, have been accepted in the absence of any substantive challenge to set out the facts of Rasputin's death, little comparative work has been carried out with the other major record of the murder, that of Vladimir Purishkevich. As a former senior Metropolitan Police detective I am amazed that in the ninety-plus years since Rasputin's murder neither academics nor researchers have taken apart the forensic evidence that confronted them. Oleg Shishkin was the first to publish the fact that the bullet to the forehead was fired at close range.[4] Many of Shishkin's other assertions are incorrect. Even the publication of the review of the original autopsy report by Professor Zharov, Russia's senior pathologist, and his colleagues failed to attract widespread attention. What concerns me to an extent is that even Zharov and his team appeared to accept the evidence of Yusupov and Purishkevich, which at a superficial level appear to corroborate each other. However, it has to be said that Zharov's remit was to consider the forensics in the case and not the circumstances of the murder. There has been no application of high-level detective skills into the murder, just the well-intentioned comments of academics and historians. Neither have the facts been subject to the forensic analysis that is now available through the enlargement of photographs on computer screens. In a modern-day British criminal court the evidence of Yusupov and Purishkevich would not hold water. I do not profess to have all the answers but what I do have and the questions that remain are laid out for you to consider.

At this stage it is necessary to introduce some recent additions to the previously acknowledged list of conspirators. They were first named in the BBC *Timewatch* documentary which introduced me to the mysteries surrounding Rasputin's death. It was while investigating the death for *Timewatch* that I first concluded that Oswald Rayner, a member of the British Secret Intelligence Service (SIS), fired the *coup de grâce* to Rasputin's forehead. These are the SIS officers who were linked to Rasputin's demise.

Samuel John Gurney Hoare, 1st Viscount Templewood (1880–1959)
Hoare was a British Conservative politician who served in various capacities in the Tory governments of the 1920s and 1930s. He was most famous for his role as Foreign Secretary. Together with French Foreign Minister Pierre Laval, he developed the so-called Hoare– Laval Agreement, which would have granted Italy considerable territorial concessions in Ethiopia (then known as Abyssinia) and put what remained of the country under Italian hegemony. The public uproar against this apparent sell-out of the Ethiopians led to Hoare's resignation as Foreign Secretary.

Hoare lost his Cabinet position and was sent off as ambassador to Spain, a position which he retained until 1944. When he returned to Britain he was raised to the peerage as Viscount Templewood. The title became extinct upon his death in 1959.

At the time of Rasputin's death he was the head of section for the British Secret Intelligence Service in Petrograd. He was not trusted by 'professional' intelligence officers so it is possible he was unsighted on the British involvement in Rasputin's assassination.

Trying to portray an organisational chart of who was in charge of whom and what within the Petrograd SIS station is complex, although Stephen Alley, Hoare's sometime deputy, assumed the head-of-station role when Hoare departed. He and the other two agents whose details follow played particular roles in the plot to kill Rasputin. However, Purishkevich, a friend of Hoare, told Hoare of the plot to 'liquidate' Rasputin in November 1916, although Hoare says he discounted the suggestion on the basis that he had heard about so many former plots and attempts to 'liquidate the affair of

Rasputin'. His friend's tone 'was so casual that I thought his words were symptomatic of what everyone was thinking and saying rather than the expression of a definitely thought-out plan'. History tells us that the Purishkevich–Hoare meeting must have taken place after 19 November 1916, the date of Purishkevich's 'Dark Forces' speech, less than a month before Rasputin's assassination. Hoare describes the suggestion made by the Tsar to the British ambassador, George Buchanan, following the murder that Rayner was involved as an 'outrageous charge', and described the story as 'incredible to the point of childishness'. Yet the ambassador had to solemnly deny these allegations at his next meeting with the Tsar. It seems clear that after Rasputin's demise Hoare was well briefed on events and was passing information to his superiors. Did he really not know what three of his operatives were doing?

Oswald Rayner (1888–1961)

Rayner was born on 29 November 1888 in Smethwick, Staffordshire. He was educated at Oriel College, Oxford from 1907 to 1910, where he read modern languages. Between 1909 and 1912 Feliks Yusupov also attended Oxford, studying at University College. We do not know how Rayner and Yusupov met, as they were in separate colleges, although not geographically far apart, but their friendship lasted a lifetime. As the details of their relationship unfold throughout this book one is drawn to conclude, given Yusupov's homosexual/ bisexual tendencies, that he and Rayner may well have at sometime been sexually involved.

In 1910 Rayner was called to the Bar and in 1915 he became a barrister in the Inner Temple. On 15 December that year he was commissioned into the British Army as a temporary lieutenant and sent to the Petrograd SIS station, where censorship was one of his duties. It is also reasonable to conclude that in addition to his abilities as a linguist his relationship with Yusupov was one of the main reasons for his being posted to Petrograd.

Soon after Rasputin's body was found, the Tsar told George Buchanan, during an audience, that he suspected 'a young Englishman, who had been a college friend of Prince Feliks Yusupov, of having been concerned with Rasputin's murder'. We will see later that Yusupov claimed that Rayner had prior knowledge of the assassination, was with him (Yusupov) the following day and accompanied him to the railway station when he was detained attempting to flee Petrograd.

In December 1917 Rayner was promoted to temporary captain. The following year he left Russia with his colleague John Scale and was appointed to Scale's new station in Stockholm. Returning to Russia in 1919, he was sent to Vladivostok and toured Siberia. He was made a Member of the British Empire (MBE) in the same year. He left the Army in 1920 and the following year was sent to Moscow as part of a trade mission.

In 1927 Rayner translated Yusupov's book *Rasputin: His Malignant Influence and His Assassination* into English.[5] His name appears on the title page of the book, acknowledging him as the translator. The *Timewatch* team were unaware of this until I showed them the actual book.

He died in 1961, leaving a son. Interestingly, before he died he destroyed all his papers. We shall never know what was in those papers but his obituary showed that the family believed he was in the Yusupov Palace on the night of Rasputin's death, and his nephew, who I interviewed, was certain that Oswald had a ring in which was inlaid one of the bullets used in the assassination, although there is no direct evidence to substantiate this claim.

Was Rayner capable of torture and murder? I am sure of it; one only has to look at the professional attachment he formed with Scale, who was in the top league of intelligence operatives and prepared to take substantial risks to achieve his aims in the service of his country.

John Scale (1882–1949)

While making the *Timewatch* programme, I had the great privilege to interview Scale's daughter Muriel, who was then in her nineties, in her home on the Black Isle in Scotland. My lasting impression after talking to her and viewing the so-called 'Scale papers' was her abiding memory of her father's hatred for Rasputin. It is easy to discredit the evidence of the elderly, especially when it relates to events so far in the past, but Muriel, now sadly deceased, impressed me as an overwhelmingly honest witness, whose memories of what her father told her were as clear as if they had been recounted yesterday. She reinforced with absolute clarity that her father was part of the plot to kill Rasputin but was intentionally not present in Petrograd at the time.

John Scale was born on 27 December 1882, in Wales. He was educated at Repton and Sandhurst. On 8 May 1901 he was commissioned as a second lieutenant with the Royal Warwickshire Regiment. He was posted to India and in 1903 promoted to lieutenant with the 87th Punjabis, and rose again, to captain, the following year.

In December 1912 he started his relationship with Russia, where in 1913 he qualified as a 1st Class interpreter. In August 1916 he was attached to the Petrograd SIS station, where Oswald Rayner was already working. His obituary states he was attached to the Tsar's staff, and this was confirmed by Muriel, who strongly suggested that Scale in fact lived in one of the imperial palaces. He was probably in some kind of liaison role, although the precise details are not clear.

A quote from Scale's papers reveals that in November 1916 he considered that 'German intrigue was becoming more intense daily' and 'the sinister influence which seemed to be clogging the war machine, Rasputin the drunken debauche influencing Russia's policy'. It is reasonable to reflect on how much of this was influenced by Rayner's close association with Feliks Yusupov rather than clinical intelligence. My inclination is that the former provided the greater motivation for these comments.

Scale was sent to Romania on 24 November to assist in a SIS operation to destroy the Romanian oil fields and corn harvest ahead of the invading German troops. Muriel was compelling during her interview when she reiterated that her father had told her he was sent to Romania because he had to be out of Russia at the time, although he was back in Petrograd by 26 January 1917. Given the clear and supportable assertions that he was involved in the plot to kill Rasputin, was this the reason for his absence from Petrograd?

Scale narrowly escaped capture by the Bolsheviks and returned to England in 1918. He was then posted to the new Stockholm station as its head, accompanied by Rayner, as we have seen, where he recruited Russian speakers to infiltrate Russia. He eventually retired in 1927 at the rank of lieutenant colonel.

Scale died aged sixty-seven on 22 April 1949.

Stephen Alley (1876–1969)

Alley was born in Moscow to English parents. His father was an engineer employed on Russian railway construction. He was educated privately in Moscow, at King's College, London (English Literature) and Glasgow University (Engineering). He joined the family firm of Alley & McLellan Engineers in London. He became a member of the Surrey Imperial Yeomanry in 1903 and in 1904 passed an examination in Russian.

He went to Russia in 1910 to help build the first heavy oil pipeline to the Black Sea. He was recruited by Military Intelligence in 1914 and sent to the Petrograd station. He was one-time deputy to Sir Samuel Hoare and became head of station after Hoare's departure.

Alley returned to England in March 1918, where he was eventually transferred to MI5. His involvement with intelligence went on for many years and on 6 April 1969 he died at the age of ninety-three.

CHAPTER TWO

PRELUDE TO MURDER

This is what Feliks Yusupov and Vladimir Purishkevich say about the build-up to Rasputin's arrival at the Yusupov Palace in the early hours of 17 December, where he was to suffer his horrific death. The accounts are as told by Yusupov and Purishkevich, in my view proven serial liars. However, they do raise a few questions: why choose the Yusupov Palace, why bring Rasputin to the palace and remove his body by the side entrance on Moika Embankment, a short distance from a police station – and why did Rasputin agree to go with Yusupov in the first place?

Yusupov's account, from *Lost Splendour*

Yusupov was staying with his brothers-in-law at Grand Duke Aleksandr Mikhailovich's palace. He spent most of 16 December preparing for examinations which were to be held next day, but managed to find time to make his final arrangements.

> I intended to receive Rasputin in the flat which I was fitting up in the Moika basement: arches divided it in two; the larger half was to be used as a dining room. From the other half, [a] staircase . . . led to my

rooms on the floor above. Halfway up was a door opening onto the courtyard . . . The walls were of grey stone, the flooring of granite. To avoid arousing Rasputin's suspicions – for he might have been surprised at being received in a bare cellar – it was indispensable that the room should be furnished and appeared to be lived in.

When I arrived, I found workmen busy laying down carpets and putting up curtains. Three large red Chinese porcelain vases had already been placed in niches hollowed out of the walls. Various objects which I had selected were being carried in: carved wooden chairs of oak, small tables covered with ancient embroideries, ivory bowls, and a quantity of other curios.

My two servants, Grigorii and Ivan, helped me to arrange the furniture. I asked them to prepare tea for six, to buy biscuits and cakes and to bring wine from the cellar. I told them that I was expecting some friends at eleven that evening, and that they could wait in the servants' hall until I rang for them . . .

Before going back to dine with my brothers-in-law, I went into the church of Our Lady of Kazan. Deep in prayer, I lost all sense of time. When I left the cathedral after what seemed to me but a few moments, I was astonished to find I had been there almost two hours. I had a strange feeling of lightness, of well-being, almost of happiness. I hurried to my father-in-law's palace where I had a light dinner before returning to the Moika.

By eleven o'clock everything was ready in the basement. Comfortably furnished and well lighted, this underground room had lost its grim look. On the table the samovar smoked, surrounded by plates filled with the cakes and dainties that Rasputin liked so much; an array of bottles and glasses stood on a sideboard. Ancient lanterns of coloured glass lighted the room from the ceiling; the heavy red damask portieres were lowered. On the granite hearth, a log fire crackled and scattered sparks on the flagstones. One felt isolated from the rest of the world and it seemed as though, no matter what happened, the events of that night would remain forever buried in the silence of those thick walls.

The bell rang, announcing the arrival of Dmitrii and my other friends. I showed them into the dining room and they stood for a little while, silently examining the spot where Rasputin was to meet his end.

I took from the ebony cabinet a box containing the poison and laid it on the table. Dr Lazovert put on rubber gloves and ground the cyanide of potassium crystals to powder. Then, lifting the top of each cake, he sprinkled the inside with a dose of poison, which, according to him, was sufficient to kill several men instantly. There was an impressive silence. We all followed the doctor's movements with emotion. There remained the glasses into which cyanide was to be poured. It was decided to do this at the last moment so that the poison should not evaporate and lose its potency. We had to give the impression of having just finished supper – for I had warned Rasputin that when we had guests we took our meals in the basement and that I sometimes stayed there alone to read or work while my friends went upstairs to smoke in my study. So we disarranged the table, pushed the chairs back and poured tea into the cups. It was agreed that when I went to fetch the *starets*, Dmitrii, Purishkevich and Sukhotin would go upstairs and play the gramophone, choosing lively tunes. I wanted to keep Rasputin in a good humour and remove any distrust that might be lurking in his mind.

When everything was ready, Yusupov put on an overcoat and pulled a fur hat down over his ears, completely concealing his face. He and Lazovert, who was disguised as a chauffeur, then went by car to collect Rasputin.

On reaching Rasputin's house, I had to parley with the janitor before he agreed to let me in. In accordance with Rasputin's instructions, I went up the back staircase; I had to grope my way up in the dark, and only with the greatest difficulty found the *starets*'s door. I rang the bell.

'Who's that?' called a voice from inside.

I began to tremble. 'It's I, Grigorii Yefimovich. I've come for you.' I could hear Rasputin moving about the hall. The chain was unfastened, the heavy lock grated. I felt very ill at ease.

He opened the door and I went into the kitchen. It was dark. I imagined that someone was spying on me from the next room. Instinctively, I turned up my collar and pulled my cap down over my eyes.

'Why are you trying to hide?' asked Rasputin.

'Didn't we agree that no one was to know you were going out with me tonight?'

'True, true; I haven't said a word about it to anyone in the house; I've even sent away all the *tainiks* [members of the secret police]. I'll go and dress.'

. . . Rasputin wore a silk blouse embroidered in cornflowers, with a thick raspberry-coloured cord as a belt. His velvet breeches and highly polished boots seemed brand-new; he had brushed his hair and carefully combed his beard. As he came close to me, I smelled a strong odour of cheap soap which indicated that he had taken pains with his appearance. I had never seen him look so clean and tidy.

'Well, Grigorii Yefimovich, it's time to go; it's past midnight.'

'There will be no one at your house but us tonight?' he asked, with a note of anxiety in his voice.

I reassured him by saying that he would meet no one that he might not care to see, and that my mother was in the Crimea.

'I don't like your mother. I know she hates me; she's a friend of Elizabeth's. Both of them plot against me and spread slander about

me too. The Tsarina herself has often told me that they were my worst
enemies. Why, no earlier than this evening, Protopopov [the Tsar's
Interior Minister] came to see me and made me swear not to go out
for a few days. "They'll kill you," he declared. "Your enemies are bent
on mischief!" But they'd just be wasting time and trouble; they won't
succeed, they are not powerful enough. But that's enough. Come on,
let's go.'

. . . Suddenly, a feeling of great pity for the man swept over me.
I was ashamed of the despicable deceit, the horrible trickery to which
I was obliged to resort. At that moment I was filled with self contempt,
and wondered how I could even have thought of such a cowardly
crime. I could not understand how I had brought myself to decide
on it.

I looked at my victim with dread, as he stood before me, quiet and
trusting. What had become of his second sight? What good did his gift
of foretelling the future do him? Of what use was his faculty for reading
the thoughts of others, if he was blind to the dreadful trap that was
laid for him? It seemed as though fate had clouded his mind, to allow
justice to deal with him according to his deserts. But suddenly, in a
lightning flash of memory, I seemed to recall every stage of Rasputin's
infamous life. My qualms of conscience disappeared, making room for
a firm determination to complete my task.

We walked to the dark landing, and Rasputin closed the door
behind him . . . We were in pitch-black darkness. I felt fingers roughly
clutching at my hand. 'I will show you the way,' said the *starets*,
dragging me down the stairs.

His grip hurt me. I felt like crying out and breaking away, but a
sort of numbness came over me. I don't remember what he said to me,
or whether I answered him; my one thought was to be out of the dark
house as quickly as possible, to get back to the light, and to free myself

from that hateful clutch. As soon as we were outside, my fears vanished and I recovered my self-control.

We entered the car and drove off. I looked behind us to see whether the police were following; but there was no one, the streets were deserted. We drove a roundabout way to the Moika, entered the courtyard and, once more, the car drew up at the side entrance. As we entered the house, I could hear my friends talking while the gramophone played 'Yankee Doodle Went to Town'.

'What's all this?' asked Rasputin. 'Is someone giving a party here?'

'No, just my wife entertaining a few friends; they'll be going soon. Meanwhile, let's have a cup of tea in the dining room.'

We went down to the basement . . . Then, at the fateful moment, I made a last attempt to persuade him to leave St Petersburg. His refusal sealed his fate. I offered him wine and tea; to my great disappointment, he refused both. Had something made him suspicious? I was determined, come what may, that he should not leave the house alive.

Yusupov and Rasputin sat down at the table and began to talk.

We reviewed our mutual acquaintances . . . and, naturally, touched on Tsarskoe Selo. 'Grigorii Yefimovich,' I asked, 'why did Protopopov come to see you? Is he still afraid of a conspiracy?'

'Why yes, my dear boy, he is; it seems that my plain speaking annoys a lot of people. The aristocrats can't get used to the idea that a humble peasant should be welcome at the Imperial Palace. They are consumed with envy and fury, but I'm not afraid of them. They can't do anything to me. I'm protected against ill fortune. There have been several attempts on my life but the Lord has always frustrated these plots. Disaster will come to anyone who lifts a finger against me.'

Rasputin's words echoed ominously through the very room in which he was to die, but nothing could deter me now. While he talked, my one idea was to make him drink some wine and eat the cakes.

Purishkevich's account, from *The Murder of Rasputin*[1]

According to the plan we had worked out, we were to have driven not to the main entrance of the Yusupov Palace, but to the small one to which Yusupov intended to bring Rasputin as well. To do so, we had first to enter the courtyard, which was separated from the street by an iron grill fence with two pairs of iron gates. According to our agreement these should have been open at this hour.

As we drove up to the palace, however, we saw that both pairs of gates were closed. Concluding that it was still too early, we maintained our speed and drove on past the palace. Then, slowing down, we circled around the Mariinskii Theatre square and returned to the Moika by way of Prachechnyi Lane. Again the gates turned out to be closed. I was beside myself.

'Let's go to the main entrance!' I shouted to Lazovert. 'I will go in through the front door and when they open the iron gates you can drive in and park the car over there by that small entrance.'

I rang. A soldier opened the door to me and, without taking off my overcoat, but looking around to see who else was in the foyer . . . I turned to the door on the left and went into the apartment occupied by Yusupov. I entered and saw all three of them sitting in the office.

'Ah!' they exclaimed in unison. '*Vous voilà*. We have been waiting for you for five minutes already. It's after midnight.'

'You could have been waiting much longer', I said, 'if I had not had the sense to come in the main entrance.' And, turning to Yusupov, I said, 'The iron gates to your side entrance are still not open.'

'Impossible,' he exclaimed. 'I will see about it right away,' and with these words he went out.

Purishkevich took off his coat. Several minutes later Dr Lazovert, dressed in his chauffeur's uniform, came in with Yusupov by way of the stairs from the courtyard. The car had been parked at the place agreed upon – by the small door in the courtyard. Then the men went out of the drawing room, through the small lobby and down the spiral staircase to the dining room.

We sat down at the round tea table and Yusupov invited us to drink a glass of tea and to try the cakes before they had been doctored. The quarter of an hour which we spent at the table seemed like an eternity to me. There was no need for any special hurry because Rasputin had warned Yusupov earlier that his various spies would not be leaving his apartment until after midnight and if Yusupov were to arrive at Rasputin's before half past twelve, he might run into Cerberus guarding the 'venerable old man'.

Once we finished our tea, we tried to give the table the appearance of having been suddenly left by a large group frightened by the arrival of an unexpected guest. We poured a little tea into each of the cups, left bits of cake and *pirozhki* on the plates, and scattered some crumbs among several of the crumpled table napkins. All of this was necessary so that Rasputin, on entering, would feel that he had frightened a gathering of ladies who had fled the dining room for the drawing room above.

Once we had given the table the necessary appearance, we got to work on the two plates of petits fours. Yusupov gave Dr Lazovert several pieces of the potassium cyanide and he put on the gloves which Yusupov had procured and began to grate poison into a plate with a knife. Then picking out all the cakes with pink cream (there were only two varieties, pink and chocolate), he lifted off the top halves and put a good quantity of poison in each one, and then replaced the tops to make them look right. When the pink cakes were ready, we placed them on the plates with the brown chocolate ones. Then, we cut up two of the pink ones and, making them look as if they had been bitten into, we put these on different plates around the table.

Lazovert then threw the gloves on the fire and we got up from the table, leaving several chairs in disorder as well, and decided to go upstairs. But, just then, I remember it clearly, the chimney began to smoke. Thick smoke filled the room and we had to spend at least another ten minutes in clearing the air. Finally everything was in order.

We went up to the drawing room. Yusupov took two phials of potassium cyanide in solution from his desk and gave one to Dmitrii Pavlovich and one to me. Twenty minutes after Yusupov had left to pick up Rasputin we were to pour these into two of the four glasses sitting behind the bottles on the table in the dining room below.

Lazovert dressed in his chauffeur's outfit. Yusupov put on his overcoat, raised his collar, and left, saying goodbye.

The noise of the car told us that they had gone and we silently began to pace up and down in the drawing room and in the lobby by the stairs which led below. It was twenty-five minutes to one. Lieutenant S. [Sukhotin] went to see if the gramophone worked and if a record was on it. Everything was ready. I took my heavy *Sauvage* [Savage automatic pistol] from my pocket . . . and placed it on Yusupov's table.

Time passed painfully slowly. We did not feel like talking. We exchanged occasional words, only asking should we smoke, or would the smoke of a cigar or cigarette drift downstairs (Rasputin did not want Yusupov to have any male guests on the night of his visit), and then we began to smoke earnestly, I my cigar, and S. and Dmitrii Pavlovich their cigarettes.

At a quarter to one Dmitrii and Purishkevich went down to the dining room and poured the potassium cyanide into two of the wine glasses, as agreed. At this point Dmitrii expressed his fear that Yusupov might, when offering cakes to Rasputin, eat a pink one in his haste or, when pouring out the wine, take one of the poisoned glasses by mistake.

'That will not happen,' I assured the grand duke firmly. 'As I see it, Yusupov is remarkable for his great composure and his presence of mind.'

Once we had finished this task, we went back upstairs, where we strained to hear the slightest sound from the street.

'They are coming,' I suddenly said in a half-whisper, moving away from the window. Lieutenant S. rushed to the gramophone and in a few seconds we heard the sound of the American march 'Yankee Doodle', a tune which haunts me even now.

An instant later we heard the dull rumble of the car already in the courtyard, and then the slamming of the car door, the stamping of feet shaking off the snow, and the voice of Rasputin saying, 'Which way, my dear?'

Then the dining room door closed behind both arrivals and after a few minutes Dr Lazovert came up the stairs to us wearing his usual clothes – he had taken off his chauffeur's fur coat, Astrakhan hat and gloves, and had left them below.

Two early witnesses to the events of 17 December

On 18 December 1916, Major General Popov of the Detached Gendarme Corps questioned Rasputin's daughter in accordance with Article 23 of the Rules on Areas Declared Governed by Martial Law. She gave the following statement.

My name is Matryona Grigor'yevna Rasputina. I am nineteen years of age, and of Christian religion. Title: peasant of Pokrovskoe village, Tyumenskii District, Tobolskaya Province. I reside at Apartment 20, 64 Gorokhovaya Street, Petrograd.

In response to the questions I state the following: on 16 December 1916 I left our apartment at 7 p.m. and returned around 11 p.m. When I was going to go to sleep my father told me that at night he was going to visit 'the little one'. When saying 'the little one' my father meant Prince Yusupov; he always called him that. Later I went to sleep and did not see whether 'the little one' arrived and whether he and my father left together. When my father told me about this visit to Yusupov he ordered me not to mention anything about it to Mariya Yevgen'yevna Golovina [one of Rasputin's 'admirers']. My father explained to me that she might tag along with them and Yusupov did not want her to visit him.

In the morning of 17 December secret political police agents arrived at our apartment and started to ask where my father was. We became anxious and called Mariya Yevgen'yevna. She told us that there was nothing to worry about if my father left with 'the little one'; they must be still asleep and Grigorii Yefimovich would return home soon. Mariya Yevgen'yevna came to our place at 11 a.m., and there were many visitors at our apartment by then. Not to make my father's disappearance public, Mariya Yevgen'yevna and I went to a fruit shop and called Prince Yusupov from there, but he had left home already. About 12 noon or 1 p.m. Prince Yusupov telephoned our apartment. I recognised his voice. Mariya Yevgen'yevna spoke to him in English. After that conversation she became extremely anxious and went home, telling us that the prince was going to visit her. In an hour my sister and I went to Mariya Yevgen'yevna's apartment, where she told us that Prince Yusupov had sworn to her that he had not picked my father up and that my father had not visited him during the night of 17 December. Later she came to our apartment with her mother and they both cried.

I saw Prince Yusupov at our apartment only once – about five or six days ago, that must be around 12 December this year. The prince has the following distinctive features: taller than average, skinny, pale, long face, large circles under the eyes, brown hair. I can't remember whether he has a moustache or a beard.

The statement was signed by Matryona and Major General Popov, and countersigned by an assistant to the clerk of the Police Department.

On the same day, Colonel Popel', also of the Detached Gendarme Corps, questioned the yard keeper at 64 Gorokhovaya Street under Article 23. He gave the following statement.

My name is Fyodor Antonovich Korshunov. I am thirty years of age, and of Christian religion. Title: peasant of Ivantsevo village, Prudovskaya Volost, Novotorzhskoi District, Tverskaya Province. I reside at 64 Gorokhovaya Street, where I am employed as a yard keeper.

In response to the questions I state the following: on the night of 16–17 December I was on duty and was outside by the gates of the building. Soon after 1 a.m. a large car arrived at the gates. The car was khaki in colour, had a canvas top and safety glass windows, and there was a spare tyre on the back. The car, which had come from the direction of the Fontanka [one of the smaller rivers in St Petersburg, whose banks were lined with many palaces], reversed and stopped. A person unknown to me got out and went straight to the wicket gate. I asked who he was visiting and he responded, 'Rasputin.' I opened the gate and said to him, 'Here is the front door,' but the stranger said that he was going to go in through the back entrance. Then he swiftly went straight to that entrance. It was obvious that the person was familiar with the layout of the building. About thirty minutes later the stranger came out together with Rasputin. They got into the car and drove off towards the Fontanka. I had not seen that person before.

Distinctive features of the stranger: above average height, medium build, about thirty years of age, small black moustache, no beard, I think no glasses, was wearing a long expensive fur coat, with fur outside, and a black hat, which I did not see well. He was wearing high boots. The driver looked slightly older than the stranger, about thirty-five years of age, had a black medium-size moustache, no beard, was wearing a black coat with lambskin collar, fur hat and long red gloves. Having left, Rasputin has not returned home.

The statement was read back to Korshunov, signed by Colonel Popel' and countersigned by an assistant to the clerk of the Police Department.

Why the Yusupov Palace?

We are told the lure for Rasputin was a meeting with Irina Yusupova, Feliks's wife. But we know that she was not in Petrograd on the night of 16–17 December. It was considered that if shots were fired in the basement dining room they were unlikely to be heard in the street. However, according to the conspirators, Rasputin was brought to the side entrance of the Yusupov Palace and his arrival would have been in view of the police post across the river. We are also told there were no staff on duty other than two hand-picked servants, and we know the palace was being renovated at the time.

Why not drive to the rear entrance with its concealed and private road out of view of the police? It leads any reasonable person to ask whether anything occurred in the yard in front of 92 Moika Embankment, next door to the palace, and, if it did, whether it was a ruse to put the police off the scent of what really happened. The police found blood in the snow covering the yard at No. 92, but was it human? Would anyone have planned to remove a body where they could be seen clearly by police? Were the conspirators that stupid?

CHAPTER THREE

SOME REPORTED VERSIONS OF RASPUTIN'S MURDER

There are four accounts of what happened to Rasputin written by the alleged conspirators: *Rasputin: His Malignant Influence and His Assassination* (1927)[1] and *Lost Splendour* (1953, reissued 2003),[2] both by Feliks Yusupov, Vladimir Purishkevich's *The Murder of Rasputin*[3] and a further account by Dr Stanislaus de Lazovert, which is to be found in the 1923 US National Alumni document *Source Records of the Great War*.[4] I do not intend to repeat in full detail the narratives that Yusupov and Purishkevich set out in their books, although in other chapters I quote both men extensively.

Grand Duke Dmitrii never wrote about the events surrounding Rasputin's murder; in fact he never talked to Feliks Yusupov after the latter spoke freely of his version of events on the night of 16–17 December 1916. As far as we know Sergei Sukhotin never wrote about the conspiracy.

Dr Stanislaus de Lazovert

According to Lazovert:

> The shot that ended the career of the blackest devil in Russian history
> was fired by my close and beloved friend, Vladimir Purishkevich,
> reactionary deputy of the Duma.
>
> Five of us had been arranging this event for many months. On
> the night of the killing, after all details had been arranged, I drove to
> the Imperial Palace in an automobile and persuaded this black devil
> to accompany me to the home of Prince Yusupov, in Petrograd. Later
> that night M. Purishkevich followed him into the gardens adjoining
> Yusupov's house and shot him with an automatic revolver. We then
> carried his riddled body in a sheet to the river Neva, broke the ice and
> cast him in.

Lazovert goes on to support the view of Yusupov in respect of
Rasputin's connection with the Germans and Austrians, and he alleges
that Rasputin was a member of an Austrian secret society, the Green
Hand. He claims that the only people involved in the assassination
were those named by Purishkevich and Yusupov. He describes the
Yusupov Palace but alleges that he drove to collect Rasputin on his
own while the other conspirators concealed themselves in the Palace
basement. He claims that he personally collected Rasputin from his
home address. This is at odds with what Purishkevich and Yusupov
say, for they claim that although Lazovert, dressed in a chauffeur's
uniform, drove Yusupov to Rasputin's address, it was Yusupov who
in fact collected him.

Lazovert goes on to describe events as follows:

Rasputin was in a gay mood. We drove rapidly to the home of the prince and descended to the library, lighted only by a blazing log in the huge chimney place. [Yusupov, by contrast, says the room was lit by electric light and makes much of the fact that after Rasputin was shot the fellow conspirators came into the room and someone knocked the light switch, plunging the room into darkness.] A small table was spread with cakes and rare wines – three kinds of the wine were poisoned and so were the cakes. The monk threw himself into a chair, his humour expanding with the warmth of the room. He told of his successes, his plots, of the imminent success of the German armies and that the Kaiser would soon be seen in Petrograd.

Lazovert's reference to the 'library' is also of interest as the other two conspirators describe in detail the 'basement dining room', and in any case the library in the Yusupov Palace is on the ground floor. Why would Lazovert refer to the venue in which he allegedly administered the cyanide as the library? Or is Lazovert thinking of Yusupov's study on the ground floor, where the conspirators are supposed to have assembled?

Lazovert then alleges that Rasputin was offered the wine and cake but that after a period of hours the poison had not taken effect. He repeats the claims that this made the conspirators believe Rasputin was superhuman and couldn't be killed. He describes how Rasputin 'glared at us with his black, black eyes as though he read our minds and would fool us'. Strangely, the accounts of Yusupov and Purishkevich have only Yusupov in the basement dining room at this time. Lazovert tells the story in the first person as if he was there throughout the event. Is this the truth or is Lazovert gilding the lily afterwards?

Lazovert also alleges that Yusupov was not alone with Rasputin when the first shot was fired:

After a time [Rasputin] rose and walked to the door. We were afraid that our work had been in vain. Suddenly, as he turned at the door, someone shot at him quickly. With a frightful scream Rasputin whirled and fell, face down, on the floor. The others came bounding over to him and stood over his prostrate, writhing body. It was suggested that two more shots be fired to make certain of his death, but one of those present said, 'No, no; it is his last agony now.'

This is not what Yusupov or Purishkevich claim; they say that Lazovert pronounced Rasputin dead. Lazovert goes on to say:

We left the room to let him die alone, and to plan for his removal and obliteration. Suddenly we heard a strange and unearthly sound behind the huge door that led into the library. The door was slowly pushed open, and there was Rasputin on his hands and knees, bloody froth gushing from his mouth, his terrible eyes bulging from their sockets. With an amazing strength he sprang towards the door that led into the gardens, wrenched it open and went out.

In the two main conspirators' published accounts Lazovert was not even in the palace when Rasputin's 'resurrection' occurred – he is supposed to have gone with Dmitrii and Sukhotin in Purishkevich's car to dispose of Rasputin's fur coat and overboots and to collect Dmitrii's car. Lazovert then claims:

As he seemed to be disappearing in the darkness, Purishkevich, who had been standing by, reached over and picked up an American revolver and fired two shots swiftly into his retreating figure. We heard him fall with a groan, and later when we approached the body he was very still and cold and – dead.

Purishkevich said four shots were fired, two of which missed.

Lazovert then alleges that Rasputin was wrapped in a sheet and taken to the water's edge, where they made a hole in the ice and dropped him through. He concludes by surmising that 'Russia had been freed from the vilest tyrant in her history; and that is all'.

Maurice Paléologue (1859–1944), the French ambassador

Despite Yusupov's claim that the conspirators were bound to keep the details of the conspiracy and murder a secret, an account appears in the diary of Maurice Paléologue dated 24 December, published in his memoirs.[5] Now, much of this is hearsay and Paléologue's account may not be as contemporaneous as the word 'diary' suggests. Be that as it may, he claims: 'From two different sources, one of which is peculiarly private and personal, I have obtained a quantity of information which enables me to reconstruct the principal phases of the murder. I am assured that the details agree with the facts so far established by the police enquiry.'

Paléologue explains that Irina was to be used as the bait to attract Rasputin to the Yusupov Palace. He names the five 'accepted' conspirators and claims that they met at eleven o'clock in a room on the first floor where supper was served (none of the four published accounts of the conspirators mention supper). Importantly, he says: 'Whatever rumour may say, there was no orgy at the Yusupov Palace that night; no ladies were present at the gathering, whether Princess R—, or Madame D—, or Countess P—, or the dancer Karalli.' This assertion has particular relevance when we consider below the evidence of Albert Stopford and the conclusions reached by Edvard Radzinskii in *Rasputin: The Final*

Word. Meanwhile, Yusupov, when interviewed by Major General Popov of the Detached Gendarme Corps on 18 December, made a statement that was even by his own later account calculated to deceive: he suggested that there was a party at the palace and it was attended by a number of 'society ladies'.

He goes on to describe Yusupov collecting Rasputin from his apartment, and it seems fairly obvious from the detail of his account that Yusupov must have been one of his informants. He then follows very closely the Yusupov version of events. But usefully he describes Rasputin's clothing: 'He had put on his best clothes, his ceremonial get-up; he was wearing wide trousers of black velvet disappearing into new top boots, a white silk blouse with blue embroidery and a sash of black satin trimmed with gold braid, which was a present from the Tsaritsa.' Compare Yusupov's description of a 'raspberry-coloured cord' around his blouse.

After describing the room briefly Paléologue claims: 'The cakes nearest to Rasputin had been poisoned with cyanide of potassium, supplied by a doctor from Obukhov Hospital, who is a friend of Prince Feliks.' This is at odds with Yusupov's claim that he acquired the cyanide from Vladimir Maklakov.

Paléologue then reiterates a very similar story to Yusupov until he claims that Yusupov said he had no revolver, whereupon Grand Duke Dmitrii offered him his. Yusupov went back to the ground floor holding the grand duke's revolver in his left hand, behind his back. Paléologue then alleges: 'As Rasputin was bending over the sacred figure, Yusupov stood on his left and fired twice into his ribs, almost point blank.' Yusupov says he fired only one shot. Of course the two shots in quick succession do coincide with the view of Professor Dmitrii Kosorotov, the initial pathologist (see Chapter 5).

Paléologue suggests that Dmitrii went to find his car and that the

other conspirators returned to the study. This contradicts Yusupov
and Purishkevich. He also claims that Yusupov collapsed on a sofa
in a dead faint, but what sofa and where? According to Paléologue,
Purishkevich seized Yusupov 'in his rough hands, shook him,
lifted him, took away his revolver and dragged him with the other
conspirators to the room on the ground floor'. He then describes how
'Purishkevich fired one bullet into [Rasputin's] neck and another
into his body, while Yusupov, now a yelling maniac, went to fetch a
bronze candlestick and battered in his victim's skull with it'. By now,
he claims, it was a quarter past two in the morning.

At the same moment, the Grand Duke Dmitrii's car drew up at the
little gate of the garden. Assisted by a servant on whom they could rely,
the conspirators wrapped Rasputin in his cloak and even put on his
overshoes, so that nothing incriminating should be left in the palace.
They lifted the body into the car, in which the Grand Duke Dmitrii, Dr
de Lazovert and Captain [*sic*] Sukhotin quickly took their places. Then
the car made for Krestovskii Island at full speed, Lazovert showing
the way. Captain Sukhotin had explored the banks on the previous
evening. On a signal from him, the car stopped by a small bridge below
which the swift current had produced a mass of ice-floes with holes
between them. Not without difficulty, the three accomplices carried
their heavy victim to the edge of a hole and threw it in the water.

While this sinister task was in progress on Krestovskii Island,
something happened at the palace on the Moika where Prince Feliks
and Purishkevich had been left alone, and were occupied in feverishly
obliterating all traces of the murder. When Rasputin left his residence
on the Gorokhovaya, an agent of the Okhrana (the Tsar's secret police
force), Tikhomirov, whose function it was to watch over the safety of
the *starets*, had immediately posted himself so as to keep an eye on the

41

Yusupov Palace. Of the preliminaries of the drama he necessarily had no knowledge. But if he could not hear the two revolver shots which wounded Rasputin, he heard those fired in the garden [i.e. the yard at No. 92] quite clearly. He began to feel uneasy and hastily went off to advise the police lieutenant at the nearest station. When they returned together, they saw a car leave the Yusupov Palace and tear away at top speed towards the Blue Bridge.

There is no mention of an agent in the four published accounts or in the statements contained in the GARF files. Paléologue claims that a police lieutenant questioned Purishkevich at the Yusupov Palace, but from the GARF files we know that it was in fact the local police constable who spoke to him.

Grand Duke Nikolai Mikhailovich (1859–1919), cousin of Nicholas II

Grand Duke Nikolai wrote an account of Rasputin's demise shortly after the murder. Much of it reads as though his informant was Yusupov. He is clear that those involved were the five conspirators mentioned in Yusupov's and Purishkevich's accounts, and he makes no mention of any women being present in the Yusupov Palace on the night of the murder.

Nikolai claims that Yusupov and Rasputin were alone in the basement room from 12.15 a.m. until 3 a.m. He reiterates the suggestion of poisoning with cyanide and then alleges:

Seeing that his plan was not working and that Rasputin was just getting gradually drunk, Feliks left him alone in the dining room and dashed upstairs to the other conspirators where he declared in a very agitated voice: 'Gentlemen, I don't understand, but the poison isn't working. Give me a revolver; we'll have to finish him off by shooting him.' It turned out that Dmitrii Pavlovich had a revolver; for some time he refused to give it to Yusupov, but eventually he was persuaded.

The next section of his account, although hearsay, is revealing when he suggests: 'Returning to the dining room, Yusupov sat right next to Rasputin and, still talking to him, fired a shot at point-blank range. The bullet entered Rasputin's lung and passed through his liver, and he fell unconscious to the floor – to all intents and purposes a dead man.' This is the only account where anyone suggests that Rasputin was seated when shot.

Nikolai states that Lazovert observed Rasputin's death throes and then goes on to describe the resurrection using terms such as 'beast' to describe Rasputin. He deals with the alleged shooting in the yard of 92 Moika Embankment by saying: 'Purishkevich fired two shots: one hit him in the back of the head, the other in the leg. Rasputin let out a groan as he fell to the ground and then started to crawl towards one of the outer gates of the Palace.' However, we know from the post mortem that there was no bullet wound to either of Rasputin's legs. Interestingly, Nikolai goes on to claim: 'Here Yusupov caught up with him and started to hit him with a rubber club until his victim finally expired.'

Baroness Sophie Buxhoeveden (1884–1956), lady-in-waiting to Alexandra

In 1928 Baroness Buxhoeveden published a biography of Alexandra,[6] which included a chapter on Rasputin's murder. After dealing with the poisoning issue Buxhoeveden suggests:

Prince Yusupov and Purishkevich then took the *starets* into an adjoining room and, as he was admiring an ancient crucifix, shot him several times in the back. Rasputin's strong frame resisted even this, and when Prince Yusupov returned to remove his body, he got up and staggered across the room. More shots were fired, this time with effect. The body was taken in a car and thrown into a hole made in the frozen Neva. The strength of the current drove the body down under the ice and it was washed ashore some days later.

She then goes on to claim, erroneously: 'The *starets* does not seem to have been dead even when he was thrown into the water, for the cords bound round his body were loosened, and his rigid hand was folded as if making the sign of the cross.'

Usefully, Buxhoeveden tells us about the newsworthiness of the event: 'In spite of the censor . . . the story of the *starets*'s disappearance got almost immediately into the press, and caused a tremendous sensation.' Her assessment of the political implications for the imperial family was: 'Though patriotic feeling was supposed to have been the motive of the murder, it was the first indirect blow at the Emperor's authority, the first spark of insurrection. In short, it was the application of lynch law, the taking of law and judgment forcibly into private hands.' She concludes by stating: 'The whole imperial family signed a petition to the Emperor, asking leave for the grand duke to stay in Petrograd on account of his health, but the Emperor refused, making a marginal note on the petition that "no one had the right to commit murder".'

Albert Stopford, diarist

Several authors have used Stopford's diary as a basis for their writings on Rasputin's death.[7] Unfortunately, Stopford is a much-discredited diarist. Little reliance can be put on anything he says and documents that purport to be genuine cannot be found in Russian archives. Stopford, who was twice married, was a homosexual and his fall from grace came as the result of a sexual encounter with a soldier in London.

In his entry for Tuesday 2 January 1917, quoting a letter to the Marchioness of Ripon, Stopford writes: 'Rasputin was killed in the Yusupov Palace about 7 a.m. Saturday, December 31.' This date is wrong; 31 December in the Gregorian calendar corresponded to 18 December in the Julian calendar and therefore Stopford should probably have written Saturday 30 December. He goes on: 'There were present Grand Duke Dmitrii Pavlovich, Feliks Yusupov, and a conservative member of the Duma, and two lady friends of Rasputin, who left, protesting, at 4 a.m., so the man had an agony of three hours. All this is from the police report which I have got.' His times are totally inaccurate based on the evidence of anyone but particularly when you consider the statements of the police witnesses contained in the GARF files. It is he that creates the 'red herring' of women being at the Yusupov Palace.

In his entry of 6 June 1917 Stopford alleges that Yusupov told him the following: 'The deed was definitely planned to take place before Friday, December 29 1916 (Gregorian), because Feliks Yusupov was to leave next day with his two young brothers-in-law, to join his wife and spend Christmas in the Crimea with her family. On the fatal night there was no "supper-party".' This is a change from his original assertion about ladies being present and does not tally with what Yusupov tells us about Irina's intended presence in Petrograd. He then goes on to claim that the police report makes it clear that two women were present. Stopford reproduces the police report as an appendix in the published version of his diary and he purports that it is a literal translation of the 'official report' handed in by the police.

It is unlikely, to the point of being beyond belief, that this document ever existed, as it would, I am certain, have found its way into the GARF files if genuine. In my view, without any evidence to the contrary, it is a forgery compiled from snippets of information gleaned from police, gossip and the newspapers. The timings in the alleged 'police report' are so completely inconsistent with those contained in the GARF witness statements that any meaningful examination shows them to be false. I rather think that police officers seeing a body removed from the palace and placed in a car which was driven away at high speed would have attracted a statement or two in the GARF papers. We also know that Stopford's timings are totally inaccurate from the time police went to the palace on the night of the murder and when Yusupov was witnessed by an officer leaving the palace.

After discussing the poisoning episode Stopford says of Yusupov:

Accordingly he went upstairs to the ground floor to borrow Purishkevich's revolver. Returning to the dining room below with the weapon held behind his back, he approached Rasputin, who was leaning over the supper-table half dazed, and, touching him on the shoulder, said, 'On the cabinet at the end of the room there is a wonderful crucifix.' Feliks Yusupov was holding the revolver in his left hand, but having Rasputin now on his right side, quickly transferred the weapon behind his back to his right hand, and then shot Rasputin at close range through the left side, below the ribs.

Stopford suggests that Purishkevich

came out into the forecourt and fired four shots at Rasputin, the number mentioned in the police report. Two of these must have missed their aim, as only two bullets hit Rasputin, one in the back of the head, and the other fired at point-blank range at his forehead. The lifeless body was picked up and carried back into the palace to await the return of the motor-car, in which, on arrival, it was placed, driven rapidly out to Krestovskii Island, and thrown into a hole in the ice of the Little Neva.

What is interesting is that this is the first time we have anyone mentioning that Rasputin had been shot 'at point-blank range at his forehead.' Of course Stopford is wrong that another bullet hit Rasputin in the back of the head. But evidence of the forehead shot was available almost straight after the post mortem.

Stopford's diary includes an appendix which, he claims, 'represents what was generally believed, up to the time of the revolution, about the death of Rasputin'. The first point of interest comes when he asserts:

So many persons being involved in the plot, rumours were bound to leak out, and as far back as Monday last it was reported that Rasputin's death might be expected at any time. It was even understood that one of the sons of the Grand Duke Konstantin had been selected by lot to perform the deed, but that he hesitated and the execution been consequently postponed. Prince Yusupov and the young princes, his brothers-in-law, together with the other imperial princes, used to assemble at night at the Yusupov Palace, and to these gatherings they frequently invited Rasputin, their object being to extract from him as much information as possible as to the doings of august personages.

There is no evidence to suggest that Rasputin had previously been to the Yusupov Palace and, as we know, it was and had been for some time undergoing restoration and was empty.

While under the influence of liquor, Rasputin would give away, not only his own secrets, but also those of the various ministerial and other political changes that have so much incensed Russian public opinion within recent months, notably the dismissal of Sazonov, the appointment of Stürmer,* and the successive and persistent failures to introduce a stable ministry of internal reforms.

In respect of the plot to murder Rasputin, Stopford then asserts: 'They accordingly invited him to meet them as usual, and, in order to allay his possible suspicions, some of Rasputin's lady friends were included in the invitation.' There is not the slightest evidence to support this. The quote below shows where in reality most of his information came from: the local press, who undoubtedly accepted any scraps of information, whether credible or not, for this major story:

> From the reports of the police investigations cited below, and from other information by reporters on the staff of the *Novoe Vremya*, it would appear that about 2.30 at night Rasputin was told he would die, and he was given the option of committing suicide or being killed. A revolver was placed in his hand, but he flatly declined to commit suicide and discharged the weapon somewhere in the direction of Grand Duke Dmitrii. The bullet smashed a pane of glass, and the sound attracted the attention of the police outside. Subsequently he was killed and his body removed to a place unknown, presumably Tsarskoe Selo.

Some authors have relied in their assessment of the evidence on the broken glass to suggest shots were fired through the window pane.

---

* Sergei Sazonov was Foreign Minister from 1910 to 1916. Boris Stürmer was Interior Minister during 1916.

Interestingly, any visit to the basement dining room would show the virtual impossibility of Rasputin having fired a bullet through one of the small, ceiling-height windows in that room. This further confusion was probably caused by the speculation about which room was the scene of the murder. But it must throw doubt on Stopford's evidence, as elsewhere he states: 'A procession of soldiers went up the Nevskii at noon. In the afternoon I visited Feliks Yusupov's. He showed me exactly where Rasputin was killed, the blood-stained polar bear skin, and how it happened.' This renders his testimony very uncertain as here he is obviously talking about the basement dining room.

Sir Basil Thomson KCB (1861–1939)

Sir Basil Thomson was born in April 1861 and died in March 1939. From June 1913 to 1921 he was an assistant commissioner in the Metropolitan Police and was responsible for 'C' Department – crime. In 1919, while remaining as an assistant commissioner, he was appointed director of intelligence at the Home Office but resigned in unclear circumstances in 1921. In 1925 he was convicted of committing 'an act in violation of public decency' and fined £5.

In 1921 Thomson wrote an article for *The Times* on Rasputin's murder, titled 'Assassins of Rasputin – Rasputin's Fate', in which he claims that his killers 'were convinced that Rasputin was engaged in a plot to persuade the Tsar to make a separate peace with Germany, and just before Christmas Rasputin is said to have revealed the whole plan in a burst of confidence. The separate peace was to be proclaimed on January 1, 1917. How true this part of the story might be I was not in a position to judge.' He continues:

Rasputin was under triple police protection. Besides the imperial detective, there was one appointed by a group of bankers and another, it is alleged, by the Germans. On the fatal evening Rasputin visited the house of Prince Youssoupoff . . . There some bottles of port and madeira specially prepared for him were set out. The wine had previously been tested upon one of the dogs that infest the courtyards of Russian houses, and the dog had died almost immediately. Rasputin drank altogether six glasses without any apparent effect, and his companion became persuaded that this sinister, herculean monk was under satanic protection. Making some excuse, he climbed the winding staircase to the room above, where his companions were assembled, and returned to the room with a revolver which they lent him. He found Rasputin leaning on his hands, and puffing as if he were not feeling well. Presently he staggered to his feet and went over to an icon. At that moment while he was standing before the icon the pistol was fired. He uttered a great cry and fell backwards on the floor.

On hearing the shot those who were waiting upstairs came down with a doctor, who examined the wound and pronounced life extinct. They then went away to make arrangements about the removal of the body, but one of them came back after a few minutes to make sure that he was really dead, for they all seemed to have believed that a satanic power had given him superhuman strength. The pulse was not beating. The man drew aside the monk's habit to feel the heart, and at that moment Rasputin with a terrible cry seized him by the throat. There was a terrible struggle, but the other succeeded in throwing him and escaping from the room. Upstairs he found a member of the Duma, who still had three cartridges left in his revolver. The two men came out on the landing and looking down saw the great bullet-head of Rasputin ascending the stairs. He was crawling up on all fours like a bear. They withdrew again into the room and saw him stagger to his feet and make for the door into the courtyard. The snow was thick upon the ground and it was dark, but they could see him against the background of snow and the second man fired three shots. Rasputin continued to run a few paces then fell close to the gateway leading into the street. He had been shot through the head.

One of the assassins was standing by the body when there came an incessant knocking at the gate . . . The police had heard the shots and had sent to inquire what was wrong. The body was lying only a few feet from the gate. Boldness was the only course, so the assassin opened the gate and took a high tone with the constable, explaining there had been a dinner party and that one of the guests had fired his revolver at a dog in the courtyard and killed it. The man went off apparently satisfied. There were now several things to do, the body had to be dragged into the house, and a dog had to be killed and laid in its place. My informant was doing this single-handed when he heard voices in the house. The same policeman had been sent back to the front door to make further inquiries. He was questioning the assassin, who had entirely lost his head and had blurted out, 'Yes, we have killed Rasputin.' My informant stepped boldly into the breach. 'Look at him,' he said. 'The wine has turned his head; when the dog was shot I said what a pity it was not Rasputin, and this friend of mine in his fuddled state has taken it literally and thinks we have done it.'

Thomson found it difficult to understand how even a Russian policeman could have accepted such an explanation, but

one has to remember that the assassination of such a personage as Rasputin, who was under direct imperial protection, was to the mind of the ordinary Russian inconceivable, and that he was questioning persons of high rank. While the police agent was recounting his visit to his superiors a car arrived and the body was taken to the bridge and dropped into the Neva, where, as we all know, it was found some three days later.

It is unclear who Thomson's 'informant' was for the above article and the story appears to be a confused mix of Yusupov's and Purishkevich's stories. However, it is known that Thomson was a member of an informal luncheon club of British intelligence officials known as the Bolshevik Liquidation Club, set up in 1919 by Stephen Alley.

CHAPTER FOUR

MOTIVES

The First World War

If, as was reported, Rasputin had strongly lobbied against the 1904–5 war between Russia and Japan under the young but weak Nicholas II, which led to ignominious defeat for the Russians, it is hardly surprising that he might also lobby against the First World War.

Russia in 1914 was in no fit state for warfare, its Minister of Defence having suggested five years before that it would not be fully ready for a modern European war until 1917. Once Austria-Hungary declared war on Serbia, hostilities in the east were inevitable. Four days later Germany declared war on Russia and the hostilities rapidly spread westwards. The First World War had started.

It was a widely held opinion that the Tsaritsa's origins made her a likely German spy and the effect of this combined with Rasputin's stance led to a belief that a conspiracy existed to make peace with the forces of Germany and Austria-Hungary. Feliks Yusupov was certainly of that view and he suggests that Rasputin may well have leaked details of Lord Kitchener's ill-fated voyage on the cruiser HMS *Hampshire* as he headed towards Russia. Yusupov was clearly under the impression that one of Kitchener's aims was to convince the Tsar to dispose of Rasputin's services. This is implicit in Yusupov's suggestion that the *Hampshire* may have been sunk on 7 May 1916 as a result of intelligence provided to the Germans by Rasputin's clique. It is also clear from his papers that John Scale believed that Rasputin was involved in dealings with the Germans. However, recent televised evidence, collected by deep sea diver wreck detectives, discredits Yusupov's suggestion and it is now clear that the *Hampshire*, sailing at night in heavy seas, hit a German mine and sank.

The Russian army was not only ill prepared for war; it was also to some extent poorly led, although an exception can be made for General Aleksei Brusilov. The main strength of the army was its vast numbers; however, against machine guns and well-organised defence its troops were soon scythed down. The Brusilov offensive in 1916 initially achieved stunning success and demolished the Austrian Fourth and Seventh Armies. Four German divisions were rushed from the Western Front to support the retreating Austrians. Unfortunately the offensive became bogged down, as Brusilov was required to support the retreating Romanian army, which had been forced to abandon parts of the country, including Bucharest, and withdraw to Moldavia.

History tells us that Aleksandr Protopopov, the Tsar's Interior Minister, met with emissaries of the Alliance (Germany, Austria and Hungary) in respect of peace negotiations. Maurice Paléologue's diary reveals this comment by George Buchanan, the British ambassador:

> So far as home affairs are concerned, he [the Tsar] leaves public opinion to be led by ministers, such as M. Stürmer and M. Protopopov, who are notoriously compromised in Germany's favour, not to mention the fact that he allows a hot-bed of Teutonic intrigues to exist in his own Palace.

Interestingly, in his memoirs Buchanan stated that although Rasputin had initially lobbied against war, once the Tsar had committed the country to hostilities he never heard Rasputin speak out. But there again he probably wouldn't have spoken freely in front of Buchanan.

However, others viewed things differently. After the February 1917 revolution, which resulted in the abdication of the Tsar and the formation of the Provisional Government, the Extraordinary Investigating Commission was set up after the February 1917 revolution to investigate matters concerning the imperial family and Rasputin. Georgii Shavelskii, archpriest of the Russian army and fleet, told the commission:

> I first talked to the former Tsar about Rasputin on 17 March 1916. I told him that rumours about Rasputin's close relationship with the Imperial Family, his great influence over high government appointments, as well as the granting of contracts and deliveries for the army, and his leaking of military secrets acquired through his association with the Tsar's family, that such rumours were rife in the army, and were causing considerable concern and damage to Imperial prestige. The Tsar listened silently, without interrupting, and when I said that Rasputin had been seen getting drunk with Jews and Germans, he remarked, 'So I have heard.' At the end of the conversation the former Tsar asked whether I had been afraid to raise such a matter with him. My relations with the Tsar were not affected by this conversation.

Many of the imperial family thought that the Tsar had lost his grip on home affairs. From the time he decided, unwisely as it happens, to take command of the Russian army at the front, domestic matters had increasingly been dealt with by the Tsaritsa, advised by 'Our Friend'. The Tsar was tired and world weary and yearned for a life without responsibility. Plot and counter-plot were discussed: either a conspiracy to remove Rasputin's influence from the Tsar and Tsaritsa, thus allowing the Tsar to function properly, if he was ever capable of doing so, or a greater plot to depose the Tsar, a powerful and potent theory. This was compounded by the reduction in power and influence that many of the extended imperial family and the nobility held as a result of Rasputin's position as the Tsarina's and thus the Tsar's chief advisor.

Paléologue's diary of 22 December notes a conversation with the President of the Council, Trepov:

> 'In short,' I said, 'it becomes increasingly clear that the present crisis is a conflict between the Emperor and the natural, official defenders of autocracy. If the Emperor does not give way, do you think we shall see a repetition of the tragedy of Paul I [regicide]?'
>
> Trepov replied, 'I am afraid so.'

We know that Dmitrii declined to be part of a plot to overthrow the Tsar. More concerning is, if Yusupov is to be believed, that some approached him to take the throne!

Yusupov's sexuality – 'A crime of passion'

Being homosexual or bisexual and in a position of power was an oxymoron in the early twentieth century. The arraignment of the Kaiser's principal advisor, Phillip, Prince of Eulenburg, in 1908 on a charge of homosexuality caused a major scandal and a fall in international prestige.

Against this background, the letters of a relative of Nicholas II, Grand Duke Konstantin Konstantinovich, show homosexual activity was not uncommon amongst the nobility.[1] Despite expressing his disgust at his own sexual activities the writer explains in a further letter how he made love to a bath house attendant and his son. Sexual acts between males were a serious criminal offence in Russia at the time, but under the guise of marriage they were relatively commonplace and clearly in many instances ignored. What is more, homosexuality and bisexuality were far from unusual amongst the royal houses of Russia and Europe more generally. It has been suggested that Grand Duke Sergei Aleksandrovich, Grand Duke Dmitrii's guardian, was gay and this is speculated as the reason that he and Ella did not have children. Whereas now in most civilised societies individuals are more or less free to be open about their sexuality this was not the case in the late nineteenth century and much of the twentieth. It is easy to imply homosexuality when a close relationship exists between two males such as Oswald Rayner and Feliks Yusupov or Yusupov and Dmitrii. However, in the case of Yusupov he provides much of the evidence upon which evidence of his sexuality may be judged.

Much has been made of Yusupov's sexuality over the years. Outwardly he was happily married with a daughter, but this superficial exterior hid a very complex and probably confused man. Whether Yusupov was gay, bisexual or merely a cross-dresser makes little difference to me, although the probability is he was gay. There is information and speculation to suggest that Yusupov had been in a sexual relationship, whether out of desire or necessity, with Rasputin.

We first hear of Yusupov's sexuality in his memoirs:

> Then one day, the truth was brutally revealed to me by a chance encounter at Contrexeville, where my mother was taking the waters.

57

I was then about twelve. I had gone out alone one evening after dinner, for a walk in the park. I happened to pass a summer house, and glancing through the window I saw a pretty young woman in the arms of a stalwart youth. A strange emotion swept over me as I watched them embracing with such obvious pleasure. I tiptoed closer to gaze at the handsome couple, who were of course unaware of my presence.

Troubled and fascinated by what I had seen, I spent a sleepless night. The next day, at the same hour, I went back to the summer house only to find it empty. I was just going home when I met the young man coming up the path. I went up to him and asked him point blank whether he had an appointment with the girl that evening. He stared at me in astonishment, then began to laugh and asked why I wished to know. When I confessed that I had watched them in the summer house, he told me he was expecting the girl at his hotel that same evening, and asked me to join them there. Imagine my feelings at receiving this invitation . . . He was sitting on the veranda waiting for me. He congratulated me on my punctuality and took me to his room, and had just begun to tell me that he was from the Argentine when his girlfriend appeared. I don't know how long I was with them . . . In my youthful ignorance, I failed to discriminate between the sexes.

Was this, as it appears to read, a bisexual encounter? Certainly Yusupov writes about his desires elsewhere in his memoirs and is open about dressing as a woman and visiting bars with a friend and talking to young male army officers.

His father, who himself appears to have been involved with a series of young male lovers, once interrupted a strange role-playing game in which Yusupov was acting out a master role with the servants in the Egyptian Room of the Yusupov Palace. Furthermore, he appeared in music hall dressed as a woman until his parents curtailed his thespian activities. Irina's parents intervened at one stage to place a sanction on their marriage and it was only Yusupov's smooth talking that allowed the engagement to continue.

Yusupov would say that as part of the plot to lure Rasputin to the palace, he forged a friendship with the person he was later to describe as 'Satan'. In *Lost Splendour* he takes us through sessions where Rasputin allegedly hypnotised him so that he was completely under his control and unaware of what was happening.

This telling extract comes from Grand Duke Nikolai Mikhailovich's diaries:

> Feliks laid out the whole story for me. Grishka [Rasputin] had taken a liking to him at once . . . and soon afterwards came to trust him, to trust him completely. They saw each other almost every other day and talked about everything and Rasputin initiated him into his schemes, not being shy at all about such revelations.
>
> I cannot understand Rasputin's psyche. How, for example, is one to explain Rasputin's boundless trust in the young Yusupov, the trust of someone who trusted no one at all, afraid that he would be poisoned or killed? It remains to propose something rather incredible, and that is that [Rasputin] was infatuated with and had a carnal passion for Feliks that darkened the strapping peasant and libertine and led him to his grave. Did they really just talk during their endless conversations? I'm convinced there were physical manifestations of friendship in the form of kisses, mutual touching, and it may be, even something more cynical. Rasputin's sadism is not open to doubt. But just how great Feliks's carnal perversions were is still little understood by me, although before his marriage there were rumours in society about his lasciviousness.

We need also to look at the relationship between Yusupov and Grand Duke Dmitrii. He was a cousin of the Tsar and by all accounts his favoured cousin. The intensity of the relationship between these two young men is vividly displayed in a letter from Dmitrii to Yusupov, after the murder but before the breakdown in their relationship. The letter may be found in full on the Alexander Palace website.

Kazvin, Persia

23 April 1917

My dear, good friend,

Yes! It [the Revolution] has happened! The development of events, the possibility of which you and I had visualised, has come to pass. The final catastrophe has been brought about by the wilful and short-sighted obstinacy of a woman [Alexandra]. It has, naturally, swept away Tsarskoe and all of us at one stroke, for now the very name of Romanov is a synonym for every kind of filth and indecency. I regard the future gloomily, and if I had not firm faith in God's mercy, and were not convinced that everything comes to an end – that better days must dawn at last – I should most likely have lost courage long ago!

. . . Ah, how desperately I long at times to have a talk with you! How intensely I long to share my thoughts and opinions with you! We have lived through so much together; it is not often that people meet under such strange conditions. You used to understand me so well; you knew how to support me in moments of trial. For God's sake write to me. What is happening? How are things?

. . . Could you not tentatively inquire what it would be advisable for me to do? Honestly speaking, I have no particular desire to come back to Russia just now; anyhow, what am I to do there? Shall I come back, and, with hands idly folded in my lap, calmly endure all sorts of filthy insinuations only because I bear the name of Romanov and am descended in a straight line from the 'Tsar liberator'? I cannot do that. Furthermore, I am firmly convinced that, should the need for my services arise, I shall not be forgotten. So I must again restrain my urgent desire to see you and to speak to you.

. . . When all is said and done, we have had some delightful times, although we have gone through trying experiences, as for example our separation. But we have had occasion for laughter too – 'Listen, If You Like' and so forth, to the accompaniment of our guitars. Yes, we have had jolly times. And my delightful rooms! My beautiful lounge with the grey divan and the tiger skin! All this is far away. I had to sell the house, as one must live somehow, and all my furniture has gone to the devil. I am sorry about my rooms.

Karalli [a ballerina and cinema actress] wrote to me about three months ago, telling me with great joy that she had heard from you. I had a telegram from her a little while ago, in which she says that she is temporarily in Petr. and that she had a long conversation with 'your friend'. Can you be this friend? She never once mentioned your name, she merely said 'your friend'.

In finishing this letter, my dear friend, I might even say without fear of exaggeration, my dearest friend, I wish to assure you of my sincerest affection. My thoughts often and often fly to you in an eager but impotent desire to help you, or only to be with you. Kiss your wife for me. She will know me better by now from your descriptions of me. I send my love to your parents. Tell your mother that I frequently think of her.

God keep you, my dear friend. Keep up your spirits. I am as yet far from losing courage. For God's sake, write to me as much as you possibly can, and with as many details as you can get in. If you disagree with me, say so outright, we shall understand each other.

Goodbye, I do not know when we shall meet again under what conditions and where.

Your truly devoted friend.

A recent analysis of Yusupov's various memoirs reached the conclusion, from this and other evidence, that Yusupov was gay or at least bisexual.[2] Edvard Radzinskii, by contrast, dismisses the plethora of suggestions that the demise of Rasputin took so long in the basement of 94 Moika Embankment because he was having sex with Yusupov.

Nevertheless, the length of time between Rasputin's arrival in the basement dining room and his being shot is difficult to explain, Yusupov and Purishkevich describing events very differently. In Purishkevich's account he was concerned that nothing appeared to be happening downstairs, and then he says:

> 'Just a minute, listen there, I think there is something amiss down there.'
> And, indeed there did seem to be a groaning sound. But it turned out to be a trick of our hearing, because a minute later the peaceful manner from one of the speakers and monosyllables, apparently from the other, was again audible from below.

Was the 'groaning' a groan of sexual gratification from Rasputin? It matters little! What is of interest, however, is this phrase from the original autopsy report: 'His genitals have been crushed.' My immediate reaction was that this injury suggested a sexual motive to the crime, or revenge for Yusupov's submission to Rasputin's sexual advances. I checked my hypothesis with a professor of forensic psychology, who concurred with me. He wrote: 'In terms of my view on the specific point you raise, based on the information available I would say that it is a perfectly plausible hypothesis that there could be a sadistic-sexual motivation to the aspect of the offending behaviour concerned.' We are told in both Yusupov's and Purishkevich's accounts that Yusupov violently assaulted Rasputin's body with a rubber-covered cosh. Was this injury caused then, as Yusupov's revenge for his defilement, or was it part of a protracted torture of Rasputin? Was it because Rasputin and others knew Dmitrii was in a bisexual relationship, or was it jealousy of Yusupov's love for Dmitrii rather than Rasputin?

CHAPTER FIVE

THE PRIMARY CRIME SCENE

The hitherto accepted version of events provides us with three crime scenes: first Feliks Yusupov's apartments in the Yusupov Palace, especially the basement dining room; secondly the yard outside 92 Moika Embankment, where Rasputin was allegedly shot by Vladimir Purishkevich; and finally Petrovskii Bridge and its environs.

The primary crime scene for Rasputin's murder and torture was allegedly the Yusupov Palace at 94 Moika Embankment and in particular the basement dining room assigned to Feliks and Irina Yusupov. But there is no independent evidence to prove that the majority of events leading to Rasputin's murder were played out in the Yusupov apartments – all we have is the accounts of the conspirators. We might conclude from photographs taken of the yard outside 92 Moika Embankment on 18 December, where a trail of blood was found starting at the side door to Yusupov's apartments, that the trail could be traced back into the palace. However, there is no forensic examination of the basement dining room, the stairs or the other apartments to assist us, nor any internal scene-of-crime photographs. I intend to investigate the scene and what both Yusupov, Purishkevich and others say happened in that room on the night of 16–17 December 1916. The room is small and I have reproduced its layout in Figure 1. I will use this to identify flaws and discrepancies in the evidence of the conspirators who committed themselves to paper.

Figure 1: The basement dining room as it is now, matching Yusupov's description

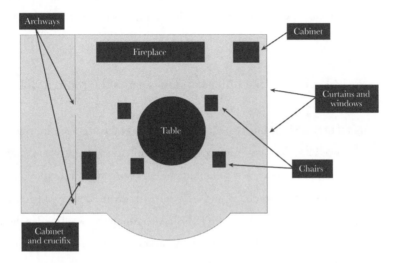

The dimensions of the basement dining room, which the Russians call a *garson'yerka*, are 7.15 metres from the fireplace to the semi-circular annex at the bottom of the room and 6.15 metres from the windows to the wall behind the two archways. Plate 1 shows the room as it was in 1916, while a recent photograph (Plate 2) shows it as it is now as part of the Yusupov/Rasputin exhibit.

This room, of which both Yusupov and Purishkevich claim to have an excellent memory, is unaccountably described differently by each. Yusupov describes it thus:

I can picture the room to this day in all its details, and I have a good reason to remember a cabinet of inlaid ebony which was a mass of little mirrors, tiny bronze columns and secret drawers. On it stood a crucifix of rock crystal and silver, a beautiful specimen of sixteenth-century Italian workmanship. On the great red granite mantelpiece were placed golden bowls, antique majolica plates and a sculptured ivory group. A large Persian carpet covered the floor and in the corner, in front of the ebony cabinet, lay a white bearskin rug. In the middle of the room stood a table at which Rasputin was to drink his last cup of tea.

Purishkevich, on the other hand, describes the room as follows:

It had been divided into two sections: one, nearer the fireplace (in which a fire was blazing brightly and cosily), was a miniature dining room, and the other, in the rear, was something in between a drawing room and a boudoir, with easy chairs and a low elegant divan, before which lay an enormous exceptionally white bearskin. Along the wall, under the windows, a small table stood in semi-darkness. On it was a tray with four unopened bottles of marsala, madeira, sherry and port, and behind these were several smoked wine glasses. On the mantelpiece, among a row of antique pieces, a crucifix of astonishing workmanship had been placed. I think that it had been chiselled from ivory.

Yusupov does describe the drawing room aspect of the room elsewhere in his memoirs but it is the positioning of the crucifix which is of considerable interest. In the basement of the Yusupov Palace the room is laid out today as in Figure 1. The crucifix is on the cabinet at the bottom left of the room, not on the mantelpiece as Purishkevich suggests. The layout of the room and the position of the crucifix have considerable importance as the tale of the murder unfolds.

Purishkevich's account continues:

Holding our breath, we went down the lobby and stood near the banister of the stairs leading below . . . It is difficult for me to determine how long we stood tensely waiting in these fixed poses by the staircase, trying neither to breathe nor move, but listening intently to literally every rustle that came from below. The voices of the speakers did reach us, sometimes as monosyllabic sounds, sometimes as snatches of conversation, but we were unable to understand what they were saying. I suppose we must have stood there on the staircase for at least half an hour, constantly rewinding the gramophone which continued to play the same old tune, 'Yankee Doodle'.

Plate 3 shows the stairs leading from the lobby outside Yusupov's study to the door into the yard and then down to the basement, each flight of stairs comprising six steps. Plate 4 shows the entrance into the basement room from the stairs, which is at the bottom left of Figure 1.

We were expecting to hear the popping of corks and Yusupov opening the bottles . . . This would have told us that things were going well and that in a few more minutes Rasputin would be a corpse. But . . . time passed. The quiet conversation continued down below and the speakers, evidently, were still not eating or drinking anything.

At last we heard the door below opening. On tiptoes we rushed noiselessly back to Yusupov's study where, a minute later, he entered. 'Just imagine, gentlemen,' he said. 'Nothing is going right. The beast will neither eat nor drink, no matter how much I urge him to warm up and accept my hospitality. What can we do?'

Dmitrii Pavlovich, in Purishkevich's account, urged Yusupov not to leave Rasputin on his own but to return downstairs, in case he came up after him and saw something he had not been expecting. Dmitrii suggested they would then either have to let Rasputin go or kill him upstairs, with uncertain consequences. Purishkevich then asked Yusupov what sort of mood Rasputin was in, to be told that he seemed to have 'some sort of premonition'. Yusupov went back downstairs at Dmitrii's behest. Eventually, after half an hour or so, Dmitrii and Purishkevich heard the popping of two corks and the clink of glasses. They listened for another quarter of an hour but still heard nothing beyond conversation and even occasional laughter. 'I do not understand this,' Purishkevich whispered. 'Can he be so enchanted that even potassium cyanide won't work on him?' Then, after a couple of minutes,

> Yusupov entered noiselessly. He was distraught and pale. 'No,' he said, 'it is impossible. Just imagine, he drank two glasses filled with poison, ate several pink cakes and, as you can see, nothing has happened, absolutely nothing, and that was at least fifteen minutes ago! I cannot think what we can do [. . .] He is now sitting gloomily on the divan and the only effect that I can see of the poison is that he is constantly belching and that he dribbles a bit. Gentlemen, what do you advise that I do?'
>
> 'Go back,' we said. 'The poison is bound to take effect finally, but if it nevertheless turns out to be useless, come back here after five minutes and we will decide how to finish him off. Time is running out. It is already very late and the morning could find us here with Rasputin's corpse in your Palace.'

Yusupov walked slowly out of the room and went downstairs. But after about five minutes he came back for the third time, saying that Rasputin was still showing no ill effects from the poison and that he was becoming extremely impatient and suspicious because of the continued non-appearance of Princess Irina. Grand Duke Dmitrii suggested calling it a day and letting Rasputin go, but Purishkevich was strongly against this. 'Your Highness, don't you understand that if he gets away today, he will have slipped away forever? Do you think that he will come to Yusupov's tomorrow once he realises that he was tricked? Rasputin cannot, must not and will not leave here alive . . . If poison doesn't work, then we must show our hand. Either we must all go downstairs together, or you can leave it to me alone. I will lay him out, either with my *Sauvage*, or I'll smash his skull in with the brass knuckles.' His account continues:

> We decided that we would all go downstairs and that I would lay him out with the brass knuckles. But, just in case, Yusupov slipped his rubber dumbbell into Lazovert's hands, though the latter assured him that he would hardly be in a position to do anything because he was so weak that he could hardly walk.
>
> This decision taken, we started carefully toward the staircase, walking in single file (with me at the head). We were already on the fifth stair when Dmitrii Pavlovich suddenly tapped me on the shoulder and whispered in my ear: '*Attendez un moment.*' . . . Lazovert, S[ukhotin] and I returned to the study where we were soon joined by Dmitrii Pavlovich and Yusupov. The latter said to me: 'V.M., will you object if, come what may, I shoot him? It will be quicker and simpler.'
>
> 'Not at all,' I replied. It is not a question of who kills him, but that he be killed, and without fail, tonight.'
>
> I had barely pronounced these words before Yusupov, with a quick, resolute stride, went to his desk and, removing his small Browning from a drawer, turned quickly and went purposefully down the stairs. We silently rushed out after him . . . knowing that now there really would not be long to wait.

Indeed, five minutes had not passed since Yusupov's departure when, after hearing two or three scraps of conversation from below, there came the dull sound of a shot, and then we heard a prolonged 'A-a-a-a!' and the sound of a body falling heavily on the floor.

In Purishkevich's account, as we have seen, Yusupov came back upstairs three times. Yusupov himself, however, claims to have returned to the study only once. His version of events unfolds as follows:

We went down to the basement . . . At the fateful moment, I made a last attempt to persuade him to leave St Petersburg. His refusal sealed his fate. I offered him wine and tea; to my great disappointment, he refused both. Had something made him suspicious? I was determined, come what may, that he should not leave the house alive.

We sat down at the table and began to talk. 'Grigorii Yefimovich,' I asked, 'Why did Protopopov come to see you? Is he still afraid of a conspiracy?'

'Why yes, my dear boy, he is; it seems that my plain speaking annoys a lot of people. The aristocrats can't get used to the idea that a humble peasant should be welcome at the Imperial Palace. They are consumed with envy and fury but I'm not afraid of them. They can't do anything to me. I'm protected against ill fortune. There have been several attempts on my life but the Lord has always frustrated these plots. Disaster will come to anyone who lifts a finger against me.'

Rasputin's words echoed ominously through the very room in which he was to die, but nothing could deter me now. While he talked, my one idea was to make him drink some wine and eat the cakes.

After exhausting his customary topics of conversation, Rasputin asked for some tea. I immediately poured out a cup and handed him a plate of biscuits [i.e. the petits fours]. Why was it that I offered him the only biscuits that were not poisoned? I even hesitated before handing him the cakes sprinkled with cyanide.

He refused them at first: 'I don't want any, they're too sweet.' At last, however, he took one, then another. I watched him, horror stricken. The poison should have acted immediately but, to my amazement, Rasputin went on talking quite calmly.

Yusupov then says that he offered Rasputin some wine. Initially Rasputin refused, but then he changed his mind. However, as with the biscuits, Yusupov gave Rasputin an unpoisoned glass. Rasputin drained it and then asked for some madeira. Yusupov made to use one of the poisoned glasses, but Rasputin insisted on using the same one.

I managed, as if by mistake, to drop the glass from which he had drunk, and immediately poured the madeira into a glass containing cyanide. Rasputin did not say anything. I stood watching him drink, expecting any moment to see him collapse. But he continued slowly to sip his wine like a connoisseur. His face did not change, only from time to time he put his hand to his throat as though he had some difficulty in swallowing. He rose and took a few steps. When I asked him what was the matter, he answered, 'Why, nothing, just a tickling in my throat. The madeira's good,' he remarked; 'give me some more.'

Meanwhile, the poison continued to have no effect, and the *starets* went on walking calmly about the room. I picked up another glass containing cyanide, filled it with wine and handed it to Rasputin. He drank it as he had the others, and still with no result. There remained only one poisoned glass on the tray. Then, as I was feeling desperate, and must try to make him do as I did, I began drinking myself. A silence fell upon us as we sat facing each other. He looked at me; there was a malicious expression in his eyes, as if to say, 'Now, see, you're wasting your time, you can't do anything to me.'

Then, suddenly, Rasputin's expression changed. Yusupov says he 'had never seen him look so terrifying. He fixed his fiendish eyes on me, and at that moment I was filled with such hatred that I wanted to leap at him and strangle him with my bare hands.' The two men sat in an ominous silence, and before long Yusupov began to suspect that Rasputin knew why he had been brought to the palace, and what the conspirators had in mind to do. 'Under Rasputin's heavy gaze, I felt all my self-possession leaving me; an indescribable numbness came over me, my head swam.'

When I came to myself, he was still seated in the same place, his head in his hands. I could not see his eyes. I had got back my self-control, and offered him another cup of tea. While I poured it, he rose and began walking up and down. Catching sight of my guitar, which I had left on a chair, he said: 'Play something cheerful, I like listening to your singing.' I found it difficult to sing anything at such a moment, especially anything cheerful . . . However, I took the guitar and sang a sad Russian ditty. He sat down and at first listened attentively; then his head drooped and his eyes closed. I thought he was dozing. When I finished the song, he opened his eyes and looked gloomily at me. 'Sing another.' . . . I sang once more but I did not recognise my own voice.

. . . The nightmare had lasted two interminable hours . . . Upstairs my friends were evidently growing impatient, to judge by the racket they made. I was afraid that they might be unable to bear the suspense any longer and just come bursting in.

Rasputin raised his head. 'What's all that noise?'

'Probably the guests leaving,' I answered. 'I'll go and see what's up.'

In my study, Dmitrii, Purishkevich and Sukhotin rushed at me, and plied me with questions. 'Well, have you done it? Is it over?'

'The poison hasn't acted,' I replied.

They stared at me in amazement. 'It's impossible!' cried the grand duke. 'But the dose was enormous! Did he take the whole lot?' asked the others.

'Every bit,' I answered.

Yusupov goes on to say that after a short discussion, he and his friends agreed to go downstairs together and strangle Rasputin. But halfway there he realised that the sudden appearance of a lot of strangers would be sure to arouse Rasputin's suspicions. Yusupov managed to convince the others, he says, that it would be best if he acted alone. He took Dmitrii's revolver and went back to the basement.

Rasputin was still sitting where Yusupov had left him, his head drooping and his breathing laboured. He asked for some wine and Yusupov poured him a glass of madeira, which revived him. Yusupov's account continues:

Suddenly he suggested that we should go to the gypsies together. I refused, giving the lateness of the hour as an excuse.

'That doesn't matter,' he said. 'They're quite used to that; sometimes they wait up for me all night [. . .] The body, too, needs a rest, doesn't it? All our thoughts belong to God, they are His, but our bodies belong to ourselves; that's the way it is!' added Rasputin with a wink.

I certainly did not expect to hear such talk from a man who had just swallowed an enormous dose of poison. I was particularly struck by the fact that Rasputin, who had a quite remarkable gift of intuition, should be so far from realising that he was near death. How was it that his piercing eyes had not noticed that I was holding a revolver behind

73

my back, ready to point it at him? I turned my head and saw the crystal crucifix. I rose to look at it more closely.

'What are you staring at that crucifix for?' asked Rasputin.

'I like it,' I replied. 'It's so beautiful.'

'It is indeed beautiful,' he said. 'It must have cost a lot [. . .] For my part, I like the cabinet better.' He went up to it, opened it and started to examine it again.

'Grigorii Yefimovich,' I said, 'you'd far better look at the crucifix and say a prayer.'

Rasputin cast a surprised, almost frightened glance at me. I read in it an expression which I had never known him to have: it was at once gentle and submissive. He came quite close to me and looked me full in the face. It was as though he had at last read something in my eyes, something he had not expected to find. I realised that the hour had come. 'O Lord,' I prayed, 'give me the strength to finish it.' Rasputin stood before me motionless, his head bent and his eyes on the crucifix. I slowly raised the revolver. Where should I aim, at the temple or at the heart? A shudder swept over me; my arm grew rigid, I aimed at his heart and pulled the trigger. Rasputin gave a wild scream and crumpled up on the bearskin. For a moment I was appalled to discover how easy it was to kill a man. A flick of the finger and what had been a living, breathing man only a second before now lay on the floor like a broken doll.

On hearing the shot Yusupov's friends rushed downstairs, but in their frantic haste they brushed against the light switch and plunged the room into darkness. At length, the light was turned on again.

Rasputin lay on his back. His features twitched in nervous spasms; his hands were clenched, his eyes closed. A blood stain was spreading on his silk blouse. A few moments later all movement ceased. We bent over his body to examine it. The doctor declared that the bullet had struck him in the region of the heart. There was no possibility of doubt: Rasputin was dead. Dmitrii and Purishkevich lifted him from the bearskin and laid him on the flagstones.

Interestingly we will see later on that if Professor Vladimir Zharov is correct there would be two bleeds onto the blouse: where the bullet entered, on the left side, and where it would have exited, in the middle of the right chest. There would also have been blood spattering, which must surely have affected the marvellous Persian carpet, yet Yusupov only seems concerned with the bearskin rug.

Yusupov states that he went upstairs only once and that he was playing his guitar and singing to Rasputin. When one considers Purishkevich's account, is it not strange that neither he nor his colleagues heard the singing or the breaking of Rasputin's unpoisoned wine glass that Yusupov says he deliberately dropped? For a group of conspirators, listening closely to every move in the basement room, are not such irreconcilable accounts unbelievable? The gramophone could have drowned out these noises – but then how could Purishkevich have heard the other small noises he mentions? What is the truth of what happened in the basement dining room before Rasputin was shot?

Lies, lies and damn lies – forensics disprove the accepted version

I deal fully with the injuries of Rasputin in Chapter 8 on his post mortem and the subsequent investigation by Professor Zharov and other leading Russian pathologists in 1993. There are, however, a number of other discrepancies that point to the falsity of the conspirators' accounts. As an investigating detective I would expect witnesses to the same event to recall the occurrence and details slightly differently. They might describe the sequence of events differently, the clothing of suspects, who said what to whom – but generally there would be overall consensus. In this case, however, the differences are of too great a consequence to be accounted for as witness error.

The car that collected Rasputin – covered or uncovered?
Purishkevich claims:

> Dr Lazovert, having bought a brush and khaki paint, and dressed in a leather apron, spent all day today on the car which will serve us tomorrow night to fetch our exalted guest. All the cars in my detachment have inscribed on them, in large red letters, my motto: '*Semper idem*'. This inscription will have to be painted over, for if by chance there should be some unfortunate turn of events, then this inscription could be the clue that could immediately lead the authorities to the Yusupov Palace and to my train. By evening the car seemed to be ready. Tomorrow it only remains to put up the top and let the drivers go off to their homes early.

He talks about when Lazovert had picked him up in the car en route to the Yusupov Palace on the night of the murder: 'I got into the car next to him and, turning towards the Kazan cathedral, we drove off along the Moika. It was absolutely impossible to recognise my car with its top up. It looked no different from the other cars we passed on the road.'

Yusupov says 'my car'; did he really mean his car or Purishkevich's car? Yusupov states that Purishkevich's car was open and that was the reason that Grand Duke Dmitrii's car was used to take Rasputin's body to the Malaya Nevka. It is strange to reflect on the care taken to paint over Purishkevich's motto on the side of his car yet he suggests that they used Dmitrii's car precisely because the police would know to whom it belonged and not stop it. Of course what would have happened if those same police had seen the grand duke depositing the body into the Nevka?

Confirmation of the fact that Yusupov arrived at Rasputin's address in a covered car is to be found in the statement of Fyodor Antonov Korshunov, the yard keeper at 64 Gorokhovaya Street. He says: 'Soon after 1 a.m. a large car arrived at the gates. The car was khaki in colour, had a canvas top and safety glass windows, and there was a spare tyre on the back.' A fuller version of this statement appears in Chapter 2.

Administering the cyanide

When it comes to adding the potassium cyanide to the petits fours, Purishkevich says the poison was grated into the pink ones. Yusupov says it was grated into the chocolate ones (in the original memoirs – 'cakes' in Lost Splendour).

A similar discrepancy occurs around the placing of the cyanide into the wine glasses. Purishkevich says that two phials of potassium cyanide solution (provided by Yusupov) were poured into two glasses only, whereas Yusupov says that granules of potassium cyanide with a little water were placed in at least three glasses (in the original memoirs; in Lost Splendour he says the cyanide was 'poured' into the glasses).

It is strange to think what might have happened if Yusupov had mistaken which petit fours were poisoned or how many glasses had cyanide in them. There could have been a poisoned, dying Yusupov and a bemused Rasputin! In fact Purishkevich tells us that Dmitrii was concerned about this very issue. Yusupov tells us he even gave Rasputin the unpoisoned cakes first and poured wine into an unpoisoned glass.

How many glasses were there to drink from? The answer according to Purishkevich is four. Yusupov says he deliberately broke the one he originally gave to Rasputin as it didn't contain cyanide. He then gave him two poisoned glasses of wine, one after the other, and states there was one poisoned glass left. But he then tells us that in order to encourage Rasputin to drink more wine he started to drink some himself, so we now have five glasses. Who was right?

The accounts regarding the preparation of the cyanide are equally complicated. Purishkevich says: 'Yusupov gave Dr Lazovert several pieces of the potassium cyanide and he put on the gloves which Yusupov had procured and began to grate the poison onto a plate with a knife.' He continues: 'We went up to the drawing room. Yusupov took two phials of potassium cyanide in solution and gave one to Dmitrii Pavlovich and one to me.' Yusupov does not confirm this account. He says: 'I took from the ebony cabinet (in the basement dining room) a box containing the poison and laid it on the table. Dr Lazovert put on rubber gloves and ground the cyanide of potassium crystals to powder.'

Was the cyanide actually ingested – did it even exist?
Purishkevich tells us that on 22 November during a cab journey Yusupov apparently told his fellow conspirators that he had obtained the potassium cyanide from Vladimir Maklakov (who always denied this). But, as we saw in Chapter 3, in what seems a very authentic, but unsubstantiated, account of the facts as told to Maurice Paléologue, it is suggested that the cyanide of potassium was 'supplied by a doctor from Obukhov Hospital, who is a friend of Prince Feliks'.

Both Yusupov and Purishkevich tell us that the cyanide was grated into the petits fours by Lazovert. Lazovert was an experienced doctor; Yusupov, according to Purishkevich, apparently provided him with gloves to wear. Where did the information come from that he should have worn gloves? Lazovert surely would have brought gloves from Purishkevich's hospital train if he knew he was to handle potassium cyanide? This points towards the cyanide with gloves being supplied to Yusupov by his doctor friend – if indeed cyanide there was.

It has been argued that either the cyanide crystals were 'past their shelf life', as potassium cyanide turns eventually to potash, or they were not in fact cyanide at all but sugar. One has to remember that Lazovert was an experienced doctor and would have known whether the poison was active or not. Interestingly, let us not forget, Yusupov tells us that they were concerned about the cyanide evaporating from the glasses, so it was left until the last possible moment to put the poison in them.

Paléologue suggests that in addition to the cyanide grated into the petit fours, 300 milligrams had been put in each of the three glasses, more than seven times what he reckons to be a fatal dose of 40 milligrams. The University of Manchester website suggests that the lowest published lethal dose for potassium cyanide is 200 milligrams and 40 milligrams for hydrogen cyanide gas. On this basis Rasputin would have consumed in the wine alone over four times the lethal dose. Add to this the amount grated into the petits fours and we have an unbelievable intake of poison. We know that Rasputin during the period before his death was drinking heavily, and alcohol, due to its acidity, speeds up the effect of potassium cyanide poisoning. Was Rasputin really a superhero who could survive such a level of poisoning? I think not.

Comparing photographs of Rasputin in his early days in St Petersburg with those taken close to the time of his demise show considerable ageing and flabbiness. Yusupov even comments on how he had aged and lost his firmness. Much of this was undoubtedly due to his debauched, drunken life-style. The following statement provides evidence that on the day before his murder Rasputin had been drinking heavily:[1]

My name is Mariya Vasil'yevna Zhuravlyova. I am twenty-eight years of age, and of Christian religion. Title: peasant of Kozlov-Bereg village, Vizheiskaya Volost, Gdovskii District, Petrogradskaya Province. I am employed as a door lady at 64 Gorokhovaya Street, where I reside.

In response to the questions I state the following: I have been employed at 64 Gorokhovaya Street for about twelve years, the last two as a door lady. On 16 December I saw Grigorii Rasputin only once, at about 3 p.m., when he returned from the bath house, where he went through the back entrance. He had not received any visitors since the morning because he was very drunk. Even when he came back from the bath house he was not quite sober. He had not more than seven visitors between 3 p.m. and midnight, they used to visit him previously as well. Only at around 10 p.m. a lady whom I never had seen before arrived and stayed with Rasputin till 11 p.m., then she left. The lady had the following distinctive features: blond hair, about twenty-five years of age, medium height, medium build. She was wearing a flared dark brown coat and same colour boots, only slightly darker, and a black hat with no veil. When I locked the front door at midnight Grigorii Rasputin was home. I don't know when he left the house and who with, because he left through the back door.

The statement was read back to the witness and signed by Colonel Popel'.

So at 3 p.m. Rasputin was not quite sober, and then he appears to have drunk heavily in Yusupov's dining room, never mind any alcohol he might have consumed in between.

Potassium cyanide gives off a characteristic smell of bitter almonds. Professor Zharov and colleagues noted that Professor Kosorotov, when carrying out the original post mortem, did not identify this smell. Zharov questions whether cyanide was ingested at all, balancing this by referring to research and experiments in 1988 by Kiliani and Erlenmeyer at Munich University which suggest that glucose can render cyanide harmless. He also refers to the work of Fisher that suggests that if cyanide is taken together with a substantial amount of carbohydrates, poisoning might not occur. My research shows that the level of glucose or carbohydrates would have to have been very high to counteract the massive amount of cyanide Rasputin ingested if the accounts of Purishkevich and Yusupov are to be accepted. But it should be noted that both Nedeljko Cabrinovic and Gavrilo Princip, respectively the attempted and actual assassin of Archduke Franz Ferdinand in Sarajevo two years earlier, tried suicide by taking cyanide and lived.

The symptoms of potassium cyanide poisoning are restlessness, dizziness, weakness, headache, tightness of the throat, laboured breathing, nausea, vomiting and rapid heart rate. These symptoms occur within minutes and in the case of a lethal dose of the poison are followed by loss of consciousness and respiratory failure, leading to death. Rasputin displayed a number of non-fatal symptoms, according to Yusupov, but most of these lesser symptoms may equally have been the product of extremely heavy drinking or alcoholic poisoning. Symptoms of alcoholic poisoning include confusion, gagging or vomiting, seizures, slow or irregular breathing, blue-tinged or pale skin, unconsciousness and slow heart rate.

Kosorotov makes the following points in respect of Rasputin: 'The cerebral matter gave off a strong smell of alcohol [and] the stomach contained about twenty soup spoons of liquid smelling of alcohol; at the moment of death the deceased was in a state of drunkenness.' Even more tellingly, he states: 'The examination of the stomach reveals no trace of poison.'

Stomach contents

Time since death can be approximated by the state of digestion of the stomach contents. It normally takes at least a couple of hours for food to pass from the stomach to the small intestine; a meal still largely in the stomach implies death shortly after eating, while an empty or nearly empty stomach suggests a longer time period between eating and death.[2] However, there are numerous mitigating factors to take into account: the extent to which the food had been chewed, the amount of fat and protein present, physical activity undertaken by the victim prior to death, the mood of the victim and physiological variation from person to person. All these factors affect the rate at which food passes through the digestive tract. Pathologists are generally hesitant to base a precise time of death on the evidence of stomach contents alone.

There is no evidence of any solids in Rasputin's stomach. By both Yusupov's and Purishkevich's accounts Rasputin was dead within two hours of consuming the petits fours. My analysis of timings against the witness-reported times of hearing the shots would mean that he was dead within ninety minutes at the latest after arriving at the Yusupov Palace. Therefore it would be reasonable to expect solids to have been discovered in the stomach contents.

Given that on the night of 17 December Maurice Paléologue was able to state that Yusupov and Grand Duke Dmitrii were the murderers and by the twenty-fourth he knew the details of the murder, it is probable that the Tsar's secret police, the Okhrana, knew the details before the post mortem. Unless someone had suggested the use of poison, would Kosorotov have commented about the lack of evidence of poison in the stomach? Analysis of post mortem samples was prohibited by imperial order.

I questioned Zharov about the lack of solids in the stomach. He was of the view that there could have been some in the soup spoons of liquid removed from Rasputin's stomach. For absolute clarity, let me repeat that Kosorotov does not refer to the presence of any solids.

There is no forensic evidence to support the conspirators' accounts that Rasputin was poisoned. It has been suggested that we might want to believe that Rasputin did ingest cyanide, but why? So much is false; why believe something for which, other than the conspirators' accounts, there is no evidence?

Whose gun?

Both Yusupov and Purishkevich concur, although Lazovert tells a different tale (to which I will return later), that at one stage Yusupov comes upstairs and the conspirators agree after discussion that he will shoot Rasputin. Yusupov says that he took Grand Duke Dmitrii's Browning, but Purishkevich says that Yusupov went to his desk drawer in the study and took out his own pocket (Baby) Browning. Another significant discrepancy in their evidence!

Yusupov goes downstairs to the basement room with the gun held behind his back. Paléologue in his diary entry of 24 December suggests Yusupov held the gun in his left hand. I have carefully trawled every picture I can find of Yusupov and from all the available evidence I am firmly of the opinion that he is right handed, and Greg King has confirmed this to me. Not that what I report now would be any different if he were left handed; it would just be in reverse. Yusupov comments that he was concerned that Rasputin would notice the gun. I suppose my question is that if he did take his Baby Browning, why did he not put it in his pocket?

A game of hide and seek?

In Figure 2 I reproduce my drawing of the basement room as it is in the Yusupov exhibition at the Yusupov Palace. Yusupov could have entered the room either through the arch at the bottom of the room (marked A as an arrowed line) or through the one at the top of the room near the fireplace (marked B as an arrowed line).

Figure 2

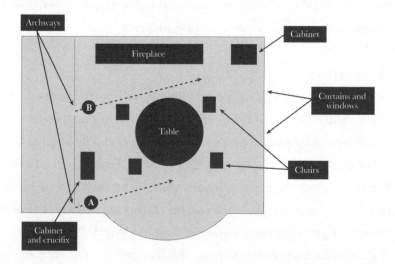

Following line A, which is the more likely entry point as it is only a few feet from the doorway leading to the staircase to the study and the side door to the yard, Yusupov, to prevent Rasputin (who we presume is sitting at the table facing the crucifix) seeing the pistol hidden behind his back (right-hand held), would have to have walked straight towards him. How did he then reach over with his left hand and pour Rasputin more wine? If the gun was in his left hand, he must have walked into the room almost side on.

Following line B, with the gun in his right hand Yusupov must have walked in sideways, left side to the fore, to avoid Rasputin's eyes. If he had it in his left hand, he would have been able to shield it from sight by a less obvious sideways walk. But again pouring the wine would have been difficult. Of course Yusupov tells us that when he entered the room Rasputin was somewhat dozy, so he might not have been fully aware of what Yusupov was up to, but another glass of wine brought him back to normal. Interestingly, Albert Stopford makes this comment: 'Feliks Yusupov was holding the revolver in his left hand, but having Rasputin now on his right side, quickly transferred the weapon behind his back to his right hand.' Why would a right-handed person hold the pistol in his left hand from the outset? As a former firearms officer I have tried to fire a revolver using my left hand (I am right handed) and it is very clumsy and difficult.

The layout of the room as described by Yusupov and Purishkevich now becomes important. Where was the crucifix – on the mantelpiece or on the cabinet at the lower end of the room, as presently arranged in the Yusupov Palace? Whether on the mantelpiece or the cabinet, Yusupov would have had to walk almost backwards at times to ensure Rasputin did not see the pistol. Yusupov tells us that Rasputin got up and walked over to the cabinet and started looking at the crucifix.

Given the small size of the dining room I now need to build some scenarios. The bullet that wounded Rasputin's left side (the first to be fired according to Kosorotov) was not fired from the front, as might be assumed by Yusupov saying that 'he came quite close to me and looked me full in the face . . . Rasputin stood before me motionless, his head bent and his eyes on the crucifix. I slowly raised the revolver. Where should I aim, at the temple or at the heart?' The post mortem photograph shows the entry point to be the left side of the chest below nipple level. From the position of the wound Rasputin's arm would have to have been raised, or strangely behind his back, at the moment the shot was fired, maybe reaching for the crucifix.

Even if Rasputin went round the table and walked towards the crucifix from the top left corner of the room as it appears in Figure 2, Yusupov could at best have stood sideways to the cabinet (initially) and then turned to face the top of the room as Rasputin came towards the cabinet. Equally, if the crucifix were on the mantelpiece Yusupov by necessity would have to be facing the right-hand wall of the room to have fired into the left side of Rasputin's body.

As an aside I also think that Yusupov indicates in his statement that he was to Rasputin's side when he wonders whether to aim at his temple, which would tend to indicate a side-on shot. Yusupov could hardly miss Rasputin. Kosorotov tells us that the bullet was fired from no more than 20 centimetres away.

Both Yusupov and Purishkevich talk of a white bearskin rug on the floor between the dining area and the lounge. They both say that Rasputin's body was on the rug and was moved by the grand duke and Purishkevich to avoid blood seeping onto the skin. This provides another anomaly: the positioning of the rug is to the bottom left of the room, and this provides some support for Yusupov's recollection of the room, with the crucifix on the cabinet in that corner of the room.

Yusupov says that Rasputin screamed and crumpled to the floor on the bearskin. Could this be possible? Yusupov, as we have discussed, was most likely at the bottom left of the room in between Rasputin and the bearskin. He was extremely close when he fired the shot (20 centimetres); he said nothing about Rasputin falling towards him, just that he crumpled. For Yusupov's version to be true Rasputin would either had to have fallen towards him or been shot from the opposite direction. The former raises the question of why Yusupov did not mention it, while the latter makes a mockery of Yusupov's evidence – looking at the crucifix and so on.

Allegedly Yusupov's fellow conspirators, on hearing the shot, rushed into the room. Dr Lazovert, having by some accounts grated potash into the cakes instead of cyanide, now allegedly made another mistake: he declared Rasputin dead! Yusupov says: 'The doctor declared that the bullet had struck him in the region of the heart. There was no possibility of doubt: Rasputin was dead.' But we are told in both Purishkevich's and Yusupov's accounts that in fact he was not dead. One has to wonder at the competence of this experienced doctor: what level of medical expertise and diagnosis were soldiers at the front receiving from him? Could he have been so incompetent, or does this go to show that the accepted version of events is substantially a lie?

So does this evidentially muddled scene provide the truth about Rasputin's demise? For so long it has been accepted as being correct, but forensic science tells us that it cannot be so. We will consider both Kosorotov's post mortem findings and Zharov's re-examination of the forensic evidence later. Suffice it to say that Kosorotov asserts and Zharov corroborates the fact that the 'second bullet' was fired shortly after the first shot and from close range.

How does this fit our conspirators' stories? Until now I have only briefly mentioned Lazovert's account of events in relation to the murder. Not much credence has been given to his short version of events in the past but it is possible to find evidence, other than forensics, to support it. The key points of his evidence are that he descended to the basement dining room with Yusupov and Rasputin – Lazovert talks about 'we', referring, I assume, to himself and his fellow conspirators – and that after a time Rasputin got up and walked to the door, whereupon 'someone shot him quickly [and] the others came bounding over . . . It was also suggested that two more shots be fired to make certain of his death. But one of those present said, "No, no; it is his last agony now."'

Paléologue also claims two shots were fired in the basement, suggesting that Yusupov fired two shots into Rasputin's back, and even Purishkevich, when postulating on whether the servants would have heard the gunfire in the yard, concludes that they would not have heard Yusupov's 'two shots' in the basement.

Interestingly, in *A Lifelong Passion* it is suggested that Yusupov sat down next to Rasputin and shot him while seated.[3] I consider this issue in Chapter 7.

Rasputin attempts escape

As we have just been discussing Lazovert's account I will introduce his evidence of Rasputin's escape from the basement first. In reading this remember that both Yusupov and Purishkevich in their accounts say that Dmitrii, Sukhotin and Lazovert had left in Purishkevich's car to dispose of Rasputin's fur coat and overboots and to collect Dmitrii's car. But Lazovert says: 'There was Rasputin on his hands and knees, the bloody froth gushing from his mouth, his terrible eyes bulging from their sockets. With an amazing strength he sprang toward the door that led into the gardens, wrenched it open and passed out.' Again it is worth highlighting that, from this evidence at least, Lazovert was in the palace with Yusupov and Purishkevich.

Yusupov says:

An irresistible impulse forced me to go down to the basement. Rasputin lay exactly where we had left him. I felt his pulse: not a beat, he was dead. Scarcely knowing what I was doing I seized the corpse by the arms and shook it violently. It leaned to one side and fell back. I was just about to go, when I suddenly noticed an almost imperceptible quivering of his left eyelid. I bent over and watched him closely; slight tremors contracted his face.

All of a sudden, I saw the left eye open . . . A few seconds later his right eyelid began to quiver, then opened. I then saw both eyes – the green eyes of a viper – staring at me with an expression of diabolical hatred. The blood ran cold in my veins. My muscles turned to stone. I wanted to run away, to call for help, but my legs refused to obey me and not a sound came from my throat. I stood rooted to the flagstones as if caught in the toils of a nightmare.

Then a terrible thing happened: with a sudden violent effort Rasputin leaped to his feet, foaming at the mouth. A wild roar echoed through the vaulted rooms, and his hands convulsively thrashed the air. He rushed at me, trying to get at my throat, and sank his fingers into my shoulder like steel claws. His eyes were bursting from their sockets, blood oozed from his lips. And all the time he called me by name, in a low raucous voice.

No words can express the horror I felt. I tried to free myself but was powerless in his vicelike grip. A ferocious struggle began. This devil who was dying of poison, who had a bullet in his heart, must have been raised from the dead by the powers of evil. There was something appalling and monstrous in his diabolical refusal to die. I realised now who Rasputin really was. It was the reincarnation of Satan himself who held me in his clutches and would never let me go till my dying day.

Nonetheless, by a 'superhuman effort' Yusupov managed to wrench himself away from the grip of Rasputin, who fell onto his back, gasping horribly and keeping hold in his hand of the epaulette he had torn from Yusupov's tunic during their struggle. The prince continues:

> For a while he lay motionless on the floor. Then after a few seconds, he moved. I rushed upstairs and called Purishkevich, who was in my study. 'Quick, quick, come down!' I cried. 'He's still alive!' At that moment, I heard a noise behind me; I seized the rubber club Maklakov had given me (he had said 'one never knows') and rushed downstairs, followed by Purishkevich, revolver in hand. We found Rasputin climbing the stairs. He was crawling on hands and knees, gasping and roaring like a wounded animal. He gave a desperate leap and managed to reach the secret door which led into the courtyard. Knowing that the door was locked, I waited on the landing above, grasping my rubber club. To my horror and amazement, I saw the door open and Rasputin disappear. Purishkevich sprang after him. Two shots echoed through the night. The idea that he might escape was intolerable!

Contrast this with Purishkevich's account:

> Some inner force pushed me toward Yusupov's desk where my *Sauvage*, which I had taken from my pocket, lay . . . I picked it up and put it back in the right hand pocket of my trousers; and . . . under the pressure of that same mysterious force, I left the study, whose hall door had been closed, and found myself in the corridor for no particular purpose.
>
> I had hardly entered the hallway when I heard footsteps below near the staircase, then the sound of the door which opened into the dining room where Rasputin lay – which the person entering evidently had not closed. Whoever could that be? I wondered, but before I had

time to give an answer, a wild, inhuman cry, which seemed to come from Yusupov, suddenly rang out: 'Purishkevich, shoot! Shoot! He's alive! He's escaping!'

Someone was rushing headlong up the stairs, screaming. It turned out to be Yusupov.

He was as white as a sheet and his fine, big blue eyes were even larger than usual and bulged out of their sockets. He was insensate and almost oblivious to my presence, and with a mad look he rushed through the door which led to the main lobby . . . I was dumbfounded for a second, but then I began to hear quite clearly from below someone's rapid, heavy footsteps making their way to the door leading to the courtyard, i.e., to that entrance from which the car had recently left.

There was not a moment to lose so, without losing my head, I pulled my *Sauvage* from my pocket, set it at *feu* [fire], and ran down the stairs. What I saw downstairs could have been a dream, had it not been so terribly real. Grigorii Rasputin, whom I had contemplated half an hour earlier, taking his last gasp heaving from side to side on the stone floor of the dining room, was now running swiftly on the powdery snow in the courtyard of the palace.

More inconsistencies

Yusupov says he rushed to his study, where he grabbed his cosh, and led Purishkevich downstairs. Purishkevich had Yusupov rushing by him into the main lobby of the palace. He makes no mention of Yusupov grabbing his cosh and going back downstairs. Yusupov even tied himself up with his own lies. He said he rushed downstairs; if he had, the next landing on which he claimed to be standing would be the one leading to the side door through which they had entered the palace. On this piece of evidence he and Purishkevich would be between Rasputin and the door to the yard. Yusupov even suggests that the side door should have been locked; who was meant to have locked it? Did Dmitrii and company go through it to take the clothing to Purishkevich's car, presumably leaving by the side gates, or did they leave by the main entrance and walk around to the yard?

Forensics confirm the lie

Purishkevich says: 'Grigorii Rasputin, whom I had contemplated half an hour earlier, taking his last gasp.' Kosorotov and Zharov confirm that either of the first two shots, the one to the stomach/liver or the one to the kidney, would have independently been fatal within fifteen to twenty minutes. According to the conspirators' accounts, half an hour after being shot, Rasputin had the strength to get up and battle to the yard; was this possible? The answer is a simple and conclusive no.

CHAPTER SIX

THE SECONDARY CRIME
SCENE, AND OTHER WITNESSES
TO THE EVENTS

Figure 3: River Moika and surrounding area

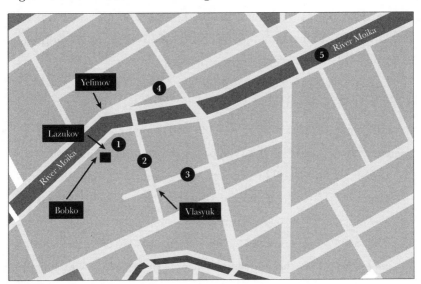

1. Yusupov Palace (92/94 Moika)

2. Prachechnyi Lane (the bridge that crosses the Moika River from Prachechnyi Lane to Bolshaya Morskaya Street is the Pochtamtskii (Post Office) Bridge)

3. Pirogov Lane, formerly Maksimilianovskii Lane

4. Bolshaya Morskaya Street

5. Blue Bridge

The yard outside 92 Moika Embankment that abuts the side wall of the Yusupov Palace and the side entrance to Feliks Yusupov's apartments is allegedly the second crime scene. I will use the witness statements of a number of people to re-examine the evidence of activity in the yard on the night of 16–17 December.

Figure 3 represents the positions of the non-conspirator witnesses who heard shots in the early morning of 17 December near the Yusupov Palace. Yefimov and Vlasyuk are police officers, whereas Bobkov and Lazukov are employees of the Yusupov family. The source of information is abstracted from witness statements in the GARF Rasputin file.

The first two witnesses I wish to introduce were both working outdoors close to the Yusupov Palace: Akim Kirillovich Lazukov, the yard keeper at 92 Moika Embankment, and Ul'yan Ivanovich Bobkov, the watchman at No. 94. Both men resided at the addresses as shown. They were Yusupov employees.

Lazukov states, when questioned by Colonel Popel':

I am employed as a yard keeper at 92 Moika. At about 2 a.m. on 17 December I started to clean the pavement next to that building. At around 3 a.m. I heard two not very loud gunshots. It seems that the sounds came from Maksimilianovskii Lane; the shooting did not take place next to No. 92 or 94. There was no car by those buildings at the time. Some time later a point duty policeman [Vlasyuk] approached me and asked whether the shooting had taken place here. I told him that I had not heard the shots here; the sounds had come from the direction of Maksimilianovskii Lane. Prince Yusupov and Buzhinskii [Yusupov's butler] did not approach us during my conversation with the point duty policeman, and the policeman did not speak to them. I have nothing more to say.

It is important to note that Lazukov, however unreliable he may be as a witness, states that there were no cars by No. 92 and 94 at the time he heard the two 'not very loud gunshots'. Interestingly, Lazukov was to tell Vlasyuk, when he spoke to him, that he had heard no shots.

Popel' also interviewed Bobkov, who stated:

I am employed as a watchman at No. 94, which belongs to Prince Yusupov. From 9 p.m. on 16 December until 6 a.m. on 17 December I was on duty by No. 94. At about 3 a.m. I heard two not very loud gunshot sounds coming from Prachechnyi Lane. I did not pay any attention to the sounds, assuming they were the sounds of frost or drain pipes. At the time when I heard those shots or cracking I was next to No. 96 and at once went to No. 94. Having checked the street near to that building and the yard of No. 92 by looking over the fence, I found nothing suspicious and went back to walk along the pavement from No. 94 to No. 96. Up to 6 a.m. I did not notice the arrival or departure of any cars to or from the front entrance of No. 94. My eyesight is extremely poor due to my war injury. I did not hear any screams following the shooting.

It must be remembered that both Bobkov and Lazukov were working on the Moika side of the palace. They both describe the noise of the shots (if you were facing the palace from the Moika) coming from the rear left-hand side of the palace, close to the rear courtyard of 94 Moika Embankment.

Two police officers heard what sounded like shots. The first was Flor Yefimov, who was on duty at the police post across the river Moika from the Yusupov Palace. He says:

During the night of 16–17 December I was on my post at Morskaya Street next to No. 61. At 2.30 a.m. I heard a gunshot, and 3–5 seconds later three more shots followed fast one after another. The sound of gunshots came from Moika, in the region of No. 92. The first gunshot was followed by a low scream, as if it was a woman's, there was no noise. In the 20–30 minutes following the shot no car or carriages went along Moika. Only half an hour later a car drove along Moika from the Blue Bridge towards Potseluev Bridge [Bridge of Kisses]; it did not stop anywhere. I reported the shots by phone to the 3rd Kazan police station and went towards the place of shooting. I noticed point duty policeman Vlasyuk at Pochtamtskii Bridge. He also had heard the gunshots and thought they were fired from Morskaya Street; he came towards me to find out who had fired the shots and where. I told him that those shots had been fired near to No. 92 Moika. Then I returned to my post and did not see or hear anything. I remember that after the shooting until five or six in the morning I did not see any other car driving along Moika, apart from the above mentioned.

It is important to note that Yefimov, whom Edvard Radzinskii relies on to suggest that a car stopped at the Yusupov Palace after the shootings, in fact says that the car travelled from the Blue Bridge, thus from right to left on the map, and 'did not stop anywhere'.

The second officer is Stepan Fedoseevich Vlasyuk, a policeman at the 3rd Kazan police station. He states:

During the night of 16–17 December I was at my post at the corner of Prachechnyi and Maksimilianovskii lanes. At about 4 a.m. I heard 3–4 gunshots soon after one another. I looked around; everywhere was quiet. I thought the sound of the shots came from the right, from the German *kirkha* [church] on Moika. I went to Pochtamtskii Bridge and called point duty policeman Yefimov, who was at his post by 61 Morskaya Street. I asked where the shots were fired from and Yefimov replied that it was on 'our side'. Then I approached the yard keeper of 92 Moika and asked him who fired the shots. The yard keeper, whose name I don't know although I know his face, replied that he did not hear any shots. At the same time I noticed, looking above the fence, that two people wearing tunics and no hats were walking along the yard of that building towards the wicket. When they approached us I recognised them: it was Prince Yusupov and his butler, Buzhinskii.

We will revisit Vlasyuk's evidence later on.

Evidential commentary

Lazukov and Bobkov were in the employ of the Yusupovs although they are mentioned nowhere in Yusupov's or Purishkevich's accounts of that evening. Lazukov was illiterate and his statement, as well as Bobkov's, was taken by Colonel Popel'. It is difficult to miss the striking similarities in the words used in both statements. However, it seems (albeit with slight time differences – and we have no idea how any or all of them knew the exact time the alleged shots were fired) that their evidence is supported by both the policemen on duty near the palace at the time, Yefimov and Vlasyuk.

Purishkevich tells us that the basement dining room would have been good if shots had to be fired as there were only two small windows at street level and thus the sound would be muffled. This could account for the 'not very loud' phrase in both statements.

The truth of Lazukov's account seems in doubt when it comes to his speaking to Vlasyuk. Vlasyuk states that Lazukov said he did not hear shots. Lazukov says that he told Vlasyuk 'that the sounds had come from the direction of Maksimilianovskii Lane.' He also says that Yusupov and Buzhinskii did not approach him and Vlasyuk at the time nor did Vlasyuk speak to them. This is contrary to the evidence of Vlasyuk and Yusupov.

Yusupov is clear in *Lost Splendour* that he spoke to Vlasyuk in the yard of No. 92; why did Lazukov lie? We shall never hear from Buzhinskii; he made no statement to the investigators and was murdered by the Bolsheviks after the revolution for failing to disclose the whereabouts of the Yusupov's hidden treasures.

Purishkevich records the following sequence in the yard:

[Rasputin] was now running swiftly on the powdery snow in the courtyard of the palace and along the iron-railed fence which led to the street, dressed in the same clothes in which I had just seem him lifeless.

At first I could not believe my eyes, but his loud cry, breaking the silence of the night, as he ran, 'Feliks, Feliks, I will tell the Tsarina everything', convinced me that it was he, that it was Grigorii Rasputin, and that he might, given his phenomenal vitality, get away. In just a few more seconds he would be through the double iron gates and on the street . . . I rushed after him and fired. In the dead silence of the night, the incredibly loud noise of my revolver shattered the air. Missed! Rasputin ran faster. I fired a second time as I ran and missed again!

Purishkevich continued to chase Rasputin across the yard. After a few seconds Rasputin reached the gates, whereupon, Purishkevich says,

I stopped, bit my left hand as hard as I could to make myself concentrate, and with one shot (the third one), hit him in the back. He stopped and this time, taking careful aim from the same spot, I fired for the fourth time. I apparently hit him in the head, for he keeled over face first in the snow, his head twitching. I ran up to him and kicked him in the temple with all my might . . . Standing over him for several minutes, I satisfied myself that there was no point in guarding him any longer. I then walked quickly back to that same little door and into the palace. I remembered clearly that in the intervals between my shots at Rasputin two men had come along the pavement on the street. The second of them, on hearing a shot, had rushed away from the fence and run off.

'What is to be done? What is to be done?' I kept saying out loud as I went into the drawing room. But there was no time to lose. 'No,' I decided, 'since things have not gone as we had planned from the very beginning, they must now take their course.' Perhaps the servants had not heard Yusupov's shots in this room, but it was impossible to imagine that the two soldiers sitting in the main entrance hall could not have heard four loud shots from my *Sauvage* in the courtyard. I walked through the lobby to the main entrance. 'Boys,' I addressed them, 'I have killed —' At these words they advanced on me in real earnest as if they wanted to seize me. 'I have killed', I repeated, 'Grishka Rasputin, the enemy of Russia and the Tsar.' At these last words, one of the soldiers became greatly agitated and rushed up to kiss me. The other said, 'Thank God, about time!'

. . . I embraced and kissed them both, and then asked them to drag Rasputin's body away from the fence in the courtyard immediately, and to put it by the stairs in the small entrance hall leading into the dining room.

This seen to, and having learned where Yusupov had gone, I went to calm him down. I found him in the brightly lit bathroom. He was leaning over the basin, holding his head with both hands, spitting repeatedly in disgust.

It is strange, then, to compare Purishkevich's recollection with that of Yusupov:

To my horror and amazement, I saw the door open and Rasputin disappear . . . Purishkevich sprang after him. Two shots echoed through the night. The idea that he might escape was intolerable! Rushing out of the house by the main entrance, I ran along the Moika to cut him off in case Purishkevich had missed him. The courtyard had three entrances, but only the middle one was unlocked. Through the iron railings, I could see Rasputin making straight for it.

I heard a third shot, then a fourth. I saw Rasputin totter and fall beside a heap of snow. Purishkevich ran up to him, stood for a few seconds looking at the body, then, having made sure that this time all was over, went swiftly into the house. I called, but he did not hear me. The quay and the adjacent streets were deserted; apparently the shots had not been heard. When I had reassured myself on this point, I entered the courtyard and went up to the pile of snow behind which lay Rasputin. He gave no sign of life. But, at that moment, I saw two of my servants running up from one side and a policeman from the other.

Vlasyuk says he saw Yusupov and the butler, but does not mention the 'two soldiers', who were in fact, as we already know, the butler, Grigorii Buzhinskii, and Ivan Nefedov, Yusupov's batman – or were they?

I went up to the policeman and spoke to him; I stood so as to make him turn his back to the spot where Rasputin lay. 'Your Highness,' he said on recognising me, 'I heard revolver shots. What has happened?'

'Nothing of any consequence,' I replied, 'just a little horseplay. I gave a small party this evening and one of my friends who had drunk a little too much amused himself by firing his revolver into the air. If anyone questions you, just say that everything's all right, and that there is no harm done!' As I spoke, I led him to the gate. I then returned to the corpse by which the two servants were standing. Rasputin's body still lay in a crumpled heap on the same spot, but his position had changed.

Plate 5 shows the absurdity of the suggestion that Vlasyuk would not have seen Rasputin's body lying on the snow through the railings of the fence or when he entered the yard.

In earlier versions of his memoirs Yusupov ran along the side of the fence with his butler. What he says is at odds with Purishkevich, although Purishkevich does say that he saw two men on the pavement, one of whom ran off on hearing the shot.

We now need to return to Vlasyuk's evidence:

When they approached us I recognised them. It was Prince Yusupov and his butler, Buzhinskii. I asked the latter who had fired the shots. Buzhinskii replied that he did not hear any shots; however, it was possible that somebody could have fired a toy pistol for fun. I think that the prince also said that he did not hear the shots. Then they left but I remained there, looked into the yard from over the fence and checked the street. When I did not find anything suspicious I went back to my post. I did not report the incident to anybody because previously I had often heard similar sounds being made by burst car tyres. About 15–20 minutes after I returned to my post, the above-mentioned Buzhinskii approached me and told me that Prince Yusupov wanted to see me.

More contradictions

We have already discussed the major inconsistencies between Yusupov and Purishkevich in relation to Rasputin's escape from the basement. Yusupov suggested that he ran to the main entrance and out onto

Moika Embankment to cut off Rasputin in case Purishkevich missed. This would have entailed turning round on the narrow basement staircase, forcing his way past the not insubstantial Purishkevich, running to the study, through the corridor to the main lobby, opening the main door and then turning right onto the embankment. One might think this would take some significant time. Purishkevich makes no mention of any of this.

Purishkevich says that he fired two shots from about twenty paces; within twenty paces Rasputin would have been at the gate. Both shots missed; he then says he bit his hand and aimed again, hitting Rasputin first in the back and then in the head as Rasputin ran away. He states that he went up to the body and kicked Rasputin's right temple. He says he was there for several minutes and does not recall Yusupov. In fact he says he found Yusupov sometime later retching in his bathroom.

Yusupov meanwhile suggested he had run along Moika Embankment parallel to the yard fence. In the original memoirs he suggested he was accompanied by his butler. To be fair Purishkevich recalled two people on the river side of the yard, one of whom ran off. Yusupov says that he shouted to Purishkevich; Purishkevich makes no mention of it. The psychology of traumatic events shows that time may, in an individual's perception, either slow down or speed up. I personally, when acting as ground commander during major public disorders in central London, experienced the almost 'slow motion' passing of time. So it is possible that Purishkevich was standing by the body for a far shorter time than he recalled.

Yusupov suggests that he stood in front of Rasputin's body so that Vlasyuk could not see it. He also suggests at the same time his two servants were running out of the palace from the side entrance. He says Vlasyuk went away and then the body was taken inside; Vlasyuk says he stayed around and checked the yard for anything suspicious.

Was the body ever actually there? Both policemen say they saw no cars returning to the yard or palace; what about Dmitrii, Sukhotin and Lazovert returning in Dmitrii's car after their abortive attempt to dispose of Rasputin's coat and boots?

Yusupov's first police interview took place on 18 December with Major General Popov of the Detached Gendarme Corps under Article 23 of the Rules on Areas Declared Governed by Martial Law. He started by identifying himself, like the other interviewees: 'My name is Feliks Feliksovich, Prince Yusupov, Count Sumarokov-El'ston. I am twenty-nine years of age, Christian religion. I reside at the palace of Grand Duchess Ksenia Aleksandrovna, Petrograd.'

He went on to explain how he had first met Rasputin about five years before at Mariya Yevgen'yevna Golovina's house, and that he met him there a few times subsequently. In November 1916, Yusupov said, Golovina persuaded him to visit Rasputin to see if he could cure the chest pains he suffered from. Rasputin's treatment improved his condition slightly but for a complete cure, we are told, Rasputin recommended a visit to some gypsy women. In his statement Yusupov continued:

Around 10 December Rasputin telephoned me and suggested that we went to the gypsies. I refused and gave him an excuse that I had to sit exams the next day. During our meetings Rasputin initiated conversations about my wife, where and how we live. He said that he wished to meet my wife; I evasively responded that a meeting could be arranged when she returned from the Crimea. However, I did not want to introduce Rasputin to my household. I had the rooms at my Moika house, No. 94, urgently refurbished and Grand Duke Dmitrii Pavlovich suggested having a house-warming party. It was decided to invite Vladimir Mitrofanovich Purishkevich, several officers and

103

society ladies to the party . . . The party was planned for 16 December. In order not to embarrass the ladies I ordered my servants to serve the tea and dinner in advance and not to enter the room later.

The majority of the guests were supposed to arrive not at the front entrance of 94 Moika, but at the side entrance by No. 92. I kept the key from that entrance on me. I arrived at around 10 p.m.; I think that I entered the apartment through the side entrance, although I can't be certain. Everything was ready for the guests in the dining room and the study. Grand Duke Dmitrii Pavlovich arrived at around 11.30 p.m., coming to the front entrance, then other guests started to arrive as well. All the ladies without doubt arrived at the side entrance; I can't remember where the male guests came to . . . At around 12.30–1.00 a.m. I went upstairs to my study in the same building and heard a telephone ring. It turned out to be Rasputin, who invited me to visit the gypsies. I replied that I was not able to come, because I had guests. Following that conversation I went downstairs into the dining room and told my guests: 'Gentlemen, Rasputin spoke to me a minute ago and invited me to visit the gypsies'. The guests cracked jokes and laughed, suggested going, but everyone stayed and continued with the dinner.

At around 2.30–3.00 a.m. two ladies decided to go home and left through the side entrance. Grand Duke Dmitrii Pavlovich left with them. When they went out I heard a gunshot in the yard, so I rang the bell and ordered one of the attendants to go and have a look. The servant returned and reported that everyone had left and there was nothing in the yard. Then I went out to the yard myself and noticed a dead dog by the fence. When I came out to the yard a person hurriedly walked away from the dog . . . I could not see him well because it was dark.

When I came back to the apartment I ordered the servant to remove the dog from the yard. I called Grand Duke Dmitrii Pavlovich straightaway and told him about the dead dog. His Imperial Highness told me that he had killed the dog. I objected and said that there was no need to do that, because it created a noise, the police would come and the fact that I was having a party with ladies in attendance would become public. Dmitrii Pavlovich replied that it was nothing and there was no need to worry. Then I called a policeman from the street and told him that if there were enquiries about the gunshots he was to tell that my friend had killed a dog. Purishkevich, who was in my study at the time, told the policeman something. I did not hear the whole conversation, I only heard him shouting that he was 'a deputy of the State Duma' and saw him waving his arms. When the grand duke told me about the killed dog he also mentioned that when he had fired the gunshot one of the ladies felt faint. I can't remember which entrance Purishkevich used when he left. I left the house at 92 Moika at about 4 a.m. and went by car to the palace of Grand Duchess Ksenia Aleksandrovna, where I live.

Yusupov then goes on to say that the following morning he intended to visit his wife in the Crimea and telephoned Golovina to tell her of his plan.

During our telephone conversation she asked me where Grigorii Yefimovich was. I replied that I didn't know because I had not seen him, only spoken to him on the phone . . . Then Golovina told me that servants at Rasputin's house confirmed that I drove Rasputin away from his apartment at around 1 a.m. However, this is a profound mistake because on 16 December I had visited Rasputin neither during the day nor during the night, and I had spent the whole night at my house at 92 Moika. My servants and my guests can confirm this.

To avoid any fatal confusion, on 17 December I considered it necessary to inform the local chief of the city police, the governor of the City of Petrograd and the Minister of Justice of everything mentioned above. The chief of police informed me that according to the policeman's statement Purishkevich had said something in my study about Rasputin's death. So I had a telephone conversation with Purishkevich about this matter and he explained that he had said something about Rasputin to the policeman, but because he had been very drunk he could not remember what exactly. I believe that those who had arranged Rasputin's assassination, if such assassination actually took place, thoroughly considered their assassination plan and deliberately linked my name and my party with this crime.

We know from Yusupov's later accounts that this was not true. We have a detailed account in his earlier recollections of Rasputin's death of having a dog shot and the blood poured on top of the stains of Rasputin's blood in the yard in order to put police dogs off the scent. The story of the dead dog is confirmed by one of Yusupov's servants, who gives us another insight into the events of the night of 16–17 December 1916. Again, he was interrogated by Major General Popov under Article 23.

My name is Ivan Grigor'yev Nefedov. I am thirty-nine years of age, I belong to the Molokan sect. Title: peasant of Rudakovo village, Betninskaya Volost, Kasimovskii District, Ryazanskaya Province. I reside in Petrograd. I am a private of the second reserve battalion, and serve as a batman of Aide-de-Camp General Prince Yusupov, Count Sumarokov-El'ston.

In response to the questions I state the following: Around 5 p.m. on 16 December 1916 the young Prince Feliks Feliksovich instructed me: 'I am going to have guests tonight. Serve the tables in the dining room downstairs for 10 p.m.,' and he left. Following that I did not see

106

the prince till later that night . . . Everything was ready for 10 p.m. Housekeeper Buzhinskii and myself took turns at the front entrance hall in No. 94, which faces the Moika. While I was on duty nobody went through the front entrance to the prince's dining room or his study. Around eleven or twelve I left the front entrance for a short while and on my return Buzhinskii told me that Grand Duke Dmitrii Pavlovich had arrived and entered the dining room downstairs. Buzhinskii and I stayed in the front entrance hall till 4 a.m. and during that time none of us entered the dining room, because the Prince had warned us that women would be among the guests and he ordered us not to enter the room. Guests arrived through the side entrance by No. 92 and entered the dining room and the prince's study from there; we could only hear the sound of the doors and gramophone music. Prince Yusupov has always kept the keys for the side entrance.

. . . On the night of 16 December I did not hear any gunshots either in the dining room or outside in the streets. About 4 a.m. I heard the bell and entered the prince's study. The guests were gone already. The prince told me to go outside to the yard and have a look at what had happened there. I went out through the side entrance to the yard of No. 92, but by that time there was nobody there and I did not notice anything unusual. I reported this to the prince. He rang the bell again few minutes later and ordered me to have a look in the yard again because there was a dead dog . . . This time I noticed a dog lying by the fence. I lifted the dog and dragged it to the garden of Yusupov's house. The dog is still there. After that the prince went out to the front hall and ordered me to call a policeman . . . The policeman entered the prince's study; I don't know the subject of their conversation. I don't know whether anybody else was present in the study at the time. Later I went to bed and did not see the prince leaving the house. I cleaned the dining room on the morning of

17 December . . . Judging by the amount of wine consumed, the guests
must have left quite drunk last night. Prince Yusupov also was tipsy that
night. The dead dog was a mongrel which used to live in Yusupov's
house. I have nothing more to say on the matter.

Yusupov tells us that Nefedov and Buzhinskii were sworn
to secrecy and therefore Nefedov's statement is a substantial lie.
However, as Yusupov is happy to name these two in *Lost Splendour*
and elsewhere, why in other places does he refer to 'two soldiers'?

The issue of the blood stains is of importance when one considers
the police photographs of the yard taken on 18 December. Plate 6
shows the side view of 94 Moika Embankment – the Yusupov Palace.
It is by that centre door that Purishkevich and Yusupov suggest the
cars were parked so the shadows would hide the identity of Rasputin,
etc. Yusupov suggests that all his fellow conspirators arrived at about
11.30 p.m. on 16 December. Nefedov certainly mentions the arrival
of Dmitrii but no one else. Purishkevich insists that he arrived in his
car which, was driven by Lazovert, at about midnight. He found
that the side gates, visible and closed in the photograph, were not
open. He claims he went to the front door at about midnight and
gained admittance, and then after a discussion Yusupov went outside
allegedly to open the side gates. Shortly afterwards he returned with
Lazovert. Yusupov and Lazovert suggest that they brought Rasputin
to the palace through the side gates.

Irrespective of the side door issue, Yusupov has all the conspirators
arriving together: 'The bell rang, announcing the arrival of Dmitrii
and my other friends.' This raises another issue: through which
door did his guests arrive? From examination of the scene-of-crime
photographs it is clear there is no bell on or near the side door leading
to Yusupov's apartments. Is Yusupov talking about the bell for the

1. The basement dining room of the Yusupov Palace as it appeared in 1916. (Museum of Political History, St Petersburg)

2. The basement dining room as it is now, as part of the Yusupov/Rasputin exhibit.

3. The stairs leading down to the basement. (Rudy de Casseres)

4. The entrance to the basement from the stairs.

5 (*below*). The yard and fence-line at 92/94 Moika Embankment. (Museum of Political History, St Petersburg)

6 (*bottom*). Side view of the Yusupov Palace. (Museum of Political History, St Petersburg)

7. The yard showing the line of blood stains.
(Museum of Political History, St Petersburg)

8. Petrovskii Bridge. (Museum of Political History, St Petersburg)

9. The fourth bridge support. (Museum of Political History, St Petersburg)

10. Petrovskii Bridge from Krestovskii Island, showing the actors' rest home.

11. Rasputin's body and what is believed to be his fur coat.
(Museum of Political History, St Petersburg)

12. Close-up of Rasputin's body. (Museum of Political History, St Petersburg)

13. Rasputin's body next to the ice hole.
(Museum of Political History, St Petersburg)

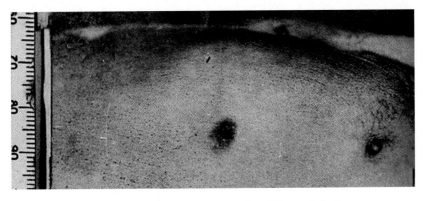

14. The bullet wound in the left side of Rasputin's chest.
(Museum of Political History, St Petersburg)

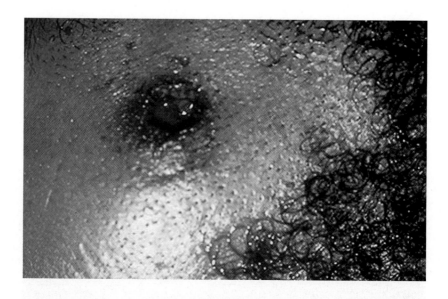

15. Control photograph showing 'sooting', evidence of a weapon fired at close range. (Suicidemethods.net)

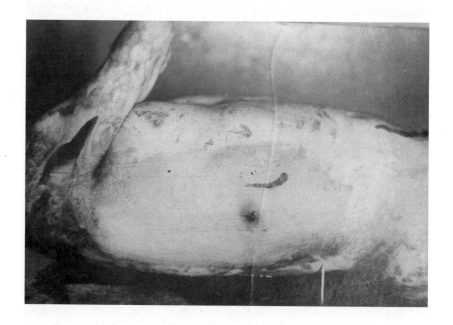

16. The bullet wound in the right side of Rasputin's back. (Museum of Political History, St Petersburg)

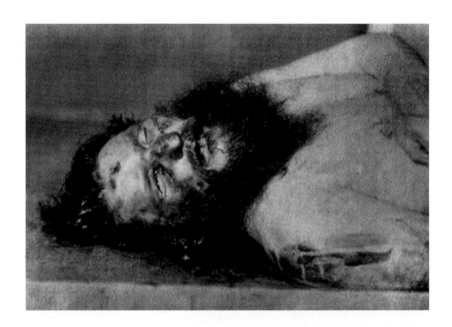

17. Post mortem photo of
Rasputin showing the bullet
wound in his forehead.
(Museum of Political
History, St Petersburg)

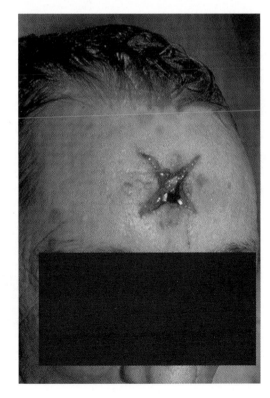

18. Control photograph
showing 'starring'.
(Suicidemethods.net)

19 & 20. The main (rear) entrance to the Yusupov Palace.
(Rob Monash)

21. The river frontage of the Yusupov Palace as it appears today.

main doors on Moika Embankment or a bell at the main courtyard entrance at the rear of the palace?

After the initial shot was fired in the basement, both Purishkevich and Yusupov suggest that Lazovert, Sukhotin and Dmitrii took some of Rasputin's clothing to be burned, and to change cars. Strangely, Yusupov suggests that when he ran out from the main entrance of the palace to pursue Rasputin as he ran across the yard, the side gates were locked and the main gates open. Who locked them? It is strange that they should have been locked if the other three conspirators were to return in Dmitrii's car to pick up Rasputin's body. Maurice Paléologue suggests that it was Dmitrii alone who had 'gone to find his car' and that the other conspirators were all present. Lazovert tends to indicate all the conspirators were present during Rasputin's attempt at escape.

Plate 7, which in fact is two photographs joined together, is revealing. On first view of these photographs in the Museum of Political History I missed something that was very important. My concentration was on the nearly straight line of red dots superimposed on the pictures that represented the blood stains laid down by Yusupov. If these dots mirrored the stains from Rasputin's blood it is amazing that a man suffering from a mortal wound, who was in Yusupov's description only capable of crawling up the stairs from the basement, should suddenly be able to run in a straight line. Purishkevich also suggests Rasputin was running and twenty paces in front of him. Paléologue, meanwhile, suggests that Rasputin was crawling in the yard, but the forensic evidence of the gunshot wounds and the range at which they were fired disproves this as well as the Yusupov/Purishkevich account.

It has been incorrectly suggested that blood does not stain snow. It does, as long as the snow does not melt or is not swept away or otherwise cleared up. In the past I have followed a trail of blood in the snow while looking for an injured animal. Stuart James and William Eckert comment that 'in cold environments bloodstain patterns deposited on snow or ice are frequently recognisable and should be preserved photographically as soon as possible'.[1]

Having now viewed the photograph(s) on a computer screen with the ability to enlarge the whole picture or sections of it I have discovered what I had initially missed. The blood line is more or less straight until it reaches a large pile of snow, where it becomes muddled. This area is some way from the main gate. The importance of this photograph is that the line of blood runs from the side door across the yard and towards the main gate. The side gates are closed and completely blocked by snow swept up from inside the yard. The photograph was taken on the eighteenth; had the yard been swept on the seventeenth or the eighteenth the blood stains found by the investigators in a near-straight line would have been swept up and muddled with the remaining snow. The fact that the investigators were able to track the blood spots means that the yard had not been swept on those days, which in turn means that the snow bank across the side gates was in place on the night of Rasputin's murder and therefore the side gates were never open that night.

The British Meteorological Office provided me with the following data from their records in respect of Petrograd:

16 December 1916: a.m. rain +2°C, p.m. snow −7°C
17 December 1916: a.m. snow −1°C, p.m. snow −6°C
18 December 1916: a.m. overcast −3°C, p.m. snow −7°C
19 December 1916: a.m. snow −7°C, p.m. snow −4°C

Purishkevich describes the snow of 16–17 December as 'light and wet'.

There is a further very important point here and I refer the reader back to the red lines marking the supposed pattern of blood staining. If these were made by Rasputin as he was escaping from his pursuers it is surprising that as he came out of the side door he deviated sharply to the left and then straightened his route towards the main gates. Yusupov tells us that only the main gates were open at this time. I would suggest that this acute deviation in direction indicates that there was an obstruction in the yard directly outside the door. This could well have been a car, but according to Yusupov and Purishkevich there was no car in the yard at this time. Bobkov and Lazukov also say there was no car in the yard.

Plate 5 also shows that the path into the yard is cleared only through the main gates and then towards the side entrance. Therefore we can say with certainty that the side gates were not used to bring Rasputin to the Moika palace or to take his body away.

But the blood stains tell us more

When Rasputin ran across the courtyard, he must have been bleeding, so a pattern of blood staining emerges. He was shot once in the back by Purishkevich, and once in the head, and collapsed in the courtyard. Purishkevich told Nefedov and Buzhinskii to drag the body across the powdery snow. They could have dragged him by the legs with his head on the ground. Did this mean more blood stains or did they in the dark follow the exact pattern of blood stains left by Rasputin as he ran across the yard? It would have been an amazing feat in the darkness of the yard to retrace Rasputin's path so carefully. Yusupov told the police in his statement that the yard was dark. Would it not have been evident to investigators that something had been dragged back to the palace? The patterns created when a bleeding body is dragged across a surface are completely different from the spotting left by someone who is bleeding but walking.

After Yusupov assaulted the body, Purishkevich describes him as being covered in blood. Yusupov says: 'As I reached the top of the stairs, I saw Rasputin stretched out on the landing, blood flowing from his many wounds.' So the body was bleeding heavily before Yusupov attacked it, which would have resulted in more blood, and Professor Zharov confirms that such an attack would lead to the attacker being covered in blood. We also have to ask which landing Yusupov means. The landing just inside the side door leading to the yard is a tiny space and realistically it would have been difficult to shroud the body in such a confined area, if not impossible. From there it is only six steps up to the landing leading to Yusupov's study; is this what Yusupov means?

The body was wrapped from top to bottom in cloth. We know its rough position from the photographs taken when the body was recovered from the Malaya Nevka: the knees were bent. Purishkevich tells us: 'We dragged Rasputin's corpse into the grand duke's car.' With a body that is bleeding heavily, the cloth would soon have been soaked, leading to more blood stains if the body was carried or dragged from the Palace to the grand duke's car. But only one path of blood stains was identified in the photograph of 18 December. So we are asked to believe that Rasputin was bleeding as he ran across the yard, and bled some more where he fell. He was then dragged back to the palace, still bleeding from his wounds, following the same path. He was attacked again in the palace and then carried out to the grand duke's car, using exactly the same path once more. A total fabrication!

The fact is that Rasputin took only one journey from the Moika basement and that was in his shroud. As he was dragged across the yard his blood marked the snow and as the conspirators opened car doors and so on, a larger stain appeared where the body rested on the snow pile.

Or did it? If, as I suggested in the *Timewatch* programme, the *coup de grâce* was delivered to Rasputin's forehead while in the yard, wrapped in the shroud, then where is the brain and skull matter that would have been blown out of the exit wound into the snow – if it had penetrated the rear of the skull that is? There is no evidence of this. I explore this in more detail in the post mortem findings.

Our two storytellers also diverge in their recollection of the timing and nature of Yusupov's attack on Rasputin's corpse once it had been carried back into the palace from the yard. Purishkevich says:

> Having learned where Yusupov had gone, I went to calm him down. I found him in the brightly lit bathroom. He was leaning over the basin, holding his head with both hands, spitting repeatedly in disgust. 'My dear, what is the matter with you? Calm down, he is already done for! I finished him off! Come with me, my dear, into your study.' Feeling obviously sick, Yusupov looked at me glassy eyed, but he obeyed. Putting my arm around his waist, I led him gingerly into his apartment. As he walked, he kept repeating: 'Feliks, Feliks, Feliks, Feliks.'

Purishkevich took Yusupov's repetition of his own name to suggest that 'something had passed between him and Rasputin in that brief moment when he had gone down to the dining room to what he had thought was a corpse. Whatever it was, it had impressed itself strongly on his brain.' He then describes how they came upon Yusupov's 'soldiers' just as they were dragging Rasputin's corpse into the vestibule at the bottom of the stairs.

Seeing what they were doing, Yusupov broke away from me and ran into his study where he grabbed the rubber dumbbell that Maklakov had given him from his desk and, returning, flung himself downstairs to Rasputin's corpse. Having poisoned him and seen that the poison didn't work, having shot him and seen that the bullet hadn't killed him, he evidently could not believe that Rasputin was already dead. He ran up to him and began to beat him on the temple with the two-pound rubber weight with all his might, in a sort of frenzy of quite unnatural excitement.

As I stood upstairs by the banister, I did not immediately understand what was happening, and then I was even more dumbfounded when Rasputin, to my great astonishment, seemed to be showing signs of life! He wheezed, and with his face turned upward, I could see quite clearly from above how the pupil of his open right eye rolled as if looking at me senselessly but horribly. I can still see this eye before me even now. I soon recovered and shouted to the soldiers to quickly pull Yusupov away from the dead man. If he and the scene were spattered with blood then, if the investigating authorities carried out a search, even without police dogs, the traces of blood would have given everything away.

The soldiers obeyed, but it cost them an extraordinary effort to restrain Yusupov who, as if mechanically, but with ever-increasing frenzy, continued to hit Rasputin in the temple. At last they pulled the prince away. Both soldiers carried him upstairs in their arms and, all covered in blood as he was, rashly sat him down in a soft leather couch in his study. It was terrible to look at him, so horrible did he look inside and out with his rolling gaze, his twitching face, and his senseless repetition of 'Feliks, Feliks, Feliks, Feliks…'.

Yusupov describes the events as follows:

My manservant then informed me that Rasputin's body had been placed on the lower landing of the staircase. I felt very ill, my head swam and I could scarcely walk. I rose with difficulty, automatically picked up my rubber club, and left the study.

As I reached the top of the stairs, I saw Rasputin stretched out on the landing, blood flowing from his many wounds. It was a loathsome sight. Suddenly, everything went black, I felt the ground slipping from under my feet and I fell headlong down the stairs. Purishkevich and Ivan found me, a few minutes later, lying side by side with Rasputin; the murderer and his victim. I was unconscious and he and Ivan had to carry me to my bedroom.

From these two accounts we can see that Purishkevich says the attack occurred before the recalled policeman, Stepan Vlasyuk, came back to the Palace. Yusupov had no recollection of assaulting the corpse but, if an attack did take place, it would have been after Vlasyuk's return. Purishkevich was worried about blood splashing from the attack upon the corpse, and splashing there would undoubtedly have been. Yusupov says he passed out and had to be taken to bed by Nefedov. Purishkevich suggests that after being dragged off Rasputin, Yusupov was fit enough and had regained his composure sufficiently to be confronted with Vlasyuk. After this violent attack Yusupov would almost certainly have been covered in blood. Yet Vlasyuk must have been a very poor policeman, because he apparently failed to notice this. Purishkevich tells us: 'Both soldiers carried him upstairs in their arms and, all covered in blood as he was, rashly sat him down in a soft leather couch in his study,' and that Vlasyuk was brought into Yusupov's study about 15–20 minutes later by my calculations. He says: 'But do you know this gentleman? I pointed to Yusupov, who was still sitting in the same position.' Vlasyuk says both men were standing.

We have a major problem in establishing what were ante mortem (before death) and what were post mortem (after death) injuries. Professor Dmitrii Kosorotov, the initial pathologist, says:

> His left side has a weeping wound, due to some sort of slicing object or a sword. His right eye has come out of its cavity and falls down onto his face . . . His right ear is hanging down and torn. His neck has a wound from some sort of rope tie. The victim's face and body carry traces of blows given by a supple but hard object. His genitals have been crushed by the action of a similar object.

Zharov correctly identifies that some of the injuries to body and face would have been caused as Rasputin's body bounced off the supports of Petrovskii Bridge. He also concludes that a number of the injuries were caused by Rasputin being hit with a cosh-type weapon.

There is a photograph showing blood stains on the fourth support of Petrovskii Bridge. However, Kosorotov is confident of the injuries to the face and genitals being caused by a blunt supple instrument – Yusupov's cosh? Injuries to genitalia often occur as the result of a deviant sexual attack; in this case were they connected with Rasputin's (unproven) sodomy of Yusupov, who willingly or otherwise submitted himself to Rasputin's sexual advances? Was it just Yusupov who attacked the body? Lazovert makes no mention of the event.

Calling Constable Vlasyuk

From Vlasyuk's statement:

> About 15–20 minutes after I returned to my post . . . Buzhinskii

approached me and told me that Prince Yusupov wanted to see me. I followed him and he took me through the front entrance to No. 94 into the prince's study. As soon as I entered the study (the study was located to the left of the front door from Moika Embankment) Prince Yusupov and a stranger walked towards me. The stranger was wearing a khaki-coloured tunic with the shoulder-pieces of an active counsellor. He had a small blond beard and moustache . . . This stranger asked me: . . . 'Do you know me?' I replied that I didn't. 'Have you heard anything of Purishkevich?' Yes. 'I am Purishkevich. Have you heard about Rasputin and do you know him?' I replied that I did not know Rasputin but had heard of him. The stranger then told me that 'he had perished and if you love the Tsar and fatherland, you have to keep quiet about it and not to tell anything to anybody . . . Now you may go.' I turned around and went back to my post. It was very quiet in the house and I did not see anybody apart from the prince, the stranger and Buzhinskii.

. . . I checked the street and the yard again, but everything was still quiet and I did not see anybody. In about twenty minutes Inspector Kalyadich approached me at my post and I told him about the incident. Then Kalyadich and me went to the front entrance of No. 94. We saw a car ready to go at the front entrance. We asked the driver whom the car was waiting for; he replied that it was for the Prince. Then Kalyadich ordered me to stay there and watch who was going to use the car and went to make his round. I recall that when we approached No. 92 Kalyadich entered the head yard keeper's room and questioned him. When he came out of the yard keeper's room I followed him to No. 94. I don't know precisely where the car had come from. Prince Yusupov alone came out of the front door (of No. 94) and drove away towards Potseluev Bridge . . . I waited by the door of that building for some time, I did not notice anyone else and returned to my post. It was shortly past 5 a.m. Kalyadich returned from his rounds in 10–15 minutes, I told him what I saw and we went to No. 94 again. We did not notice anyone there other than the duty yard keeper. Then Kalyadich went to the police station and I remained there. At about 6 a.m. he returned again and called me to go and see Colonel Rogov [a police officer], who we were supposed to report the incident to. Then I went home.

The car belonged to the prince; he had always been using it. I know this car well; it's small and brown in colour. I had not noticed any signs of a murder, and explained the conversation with the stranger in the study as some kind of test of my knowledge of my responsibilities, meaning a test of my actions following such an announcement. I did not notice that the prince or the stranger showed any signs of anxiety or embarrassment, only the stranger talked. I can't tell for sure whether they were sober.

Purishkevich recalls it thus:

One of them set off to carry out my orders, but I called the other upstairs a few minutes later and, having heard from him that the policeman on duty at the corner of Prachechnyi and Maksimilianovskii lanes had come to find out what the shooting had been about, and that when he went off duty in half an hour he would have to report what had happened in his district to his superior, I told him to bring this policeman to me.

Ten minutes later the soldier led the policeman into the study. I quickly looked him over from head to foot and at once realised that I had made a mistake in calling him in; he was a veteran of the old school. Nevertheless, I had to deal with things as they were. 'Officer,' I addressed him, 'did you come here a little while ago to inquire about what had happened and why there had been a shooting?'

'That is right, Your Excellency,' he replied.

Purishkevich then established that the solider knew who he and
Yusupov were. His account carries on:

'Listen, brother,' I continued, putting my arm around his shoulder,
'answer me honestly: do you love our holy Tsar and Mother Russia?
Do you want the victory of Russian arms over the Germans?'

'Of course, Your Excellency,' he replied.

. . . 'And do you know', I went on, 'who is the most evil enemy of
the Tsar and of Russia, who hinders our war effort, who puts Stürmers
and all sorts of Germans in the government, and who controls the
Tsarina and, through her, makes short work of Russia?'

The policeman's face brightened immediately. 'Yes,' he said,
'I know. Grishka Rasputin!'

'Well, old boy, he is no more. We killed him. It was him we were
shooting at just now. You heard, but if anyone asks you, you can say:
"I saw nothing and I know nothing." Can you manage to be quiet and
not betray us?'

The policeman became thoughtful. 'It's like this, Your Excellency.
If they ask me, and I am not under oath, then I will say nothing, but if
they put me under oath, then it can't be helped, I will have to tell the
whole truth. It would be a sin to lie.'

I realised that talking would lead nowhere and, learning that his
duty was up in half an hour and that his district chief was Lieutenant
Grigor'yev (who was, as far as I knew, a very decent fellow of good
family), I let him go in peace, deciding to leave the future to fate.

And Yusupov says:

We had scarcely reached it [Yusupov's study] when my manservant
came to say that the policeman I had talked to a few moments before

wished to see me again. The shots, it seems, had been heard from the police station, and my constable, whose beat it was, had been sent for to make a report on what had happened. As his version of the affair was considered unsatisfactory, the police insisted on fuller details. When the constable entered the room, Purishkevich addressed him in a loud voice: 'Have you ever heard of Rasputin? The man who plotted to ruin our country, the Tsar and your brother soldiers? The man who betrayed us to Germany, do you hear?'

Not understanding what was expected of him, the policeman remained silent.

'Do you know who I am?' continued Purishkevich. 'I am Vladimir Mitrofanovich Purishkevich, member of the Duma. The shots you heard killed Rasputin. If you love your country and your Tsar, you'll keep your mouth shut.'

I listened with horror to this amazing statement, which came so unexpectedly that I had no chance to interrupt. Purishkevich was in such a state of excitement that he did not realise what he was saying. Finally, the policeman spoke: 'You did right and I won't say a word unless I'm put on oath. I would then have to tell the truth as it would be a sin to lie.' Purishkevich followed him out.

Paléologue suggests that an Okhrana spy had been keeping Rasputin under surveillance and was concerned when he heard the shots. There is no surviving evidence to suggest that Rasputin was under 24-hour surveillance at the time.

CHAPTER SEVEN

THE TERTIARY CRIME SCENE

This is the only scene for which there is conclusive forensic evidence, including the recovery of Rasputin's body, the recovery of an overshoe and his coat, together with evidence of blood staining on one of the bridge supports close to where the overshoe was found. I want to clear up one issue before commencing this chapter: as the GARF statements are written it can appear that both an overshoe and a shoe were found on the ice near the bridge support. This is not correct; an overshoe only was found. Rasputin when examined at the post mortem was wearing his boots, so neither was missing and as he was wrapped in a cloth and secured with a rope, it would have not been possible for one of his shoes to fall off.

Petrovskii Bridge was built in 1839. Today it is open only to pedestrians, but at the time of Rasputin's murder it was a road bridge capable of taking two-way vehicular traffic. It is 300 metres long and runs between Petrovskii and Krestovskii islands across the Malaya Nevka (see Figure 4). The side of the bridge over which Rasputin was thrown into the river, the aspect facing the Gulf of Finland, remains intact. The other side of the bridge was demolished and rebuilt in a narrower form. The original supports still remain, surrounded, as is common among wooden-piered bridges in St Petersburg, with strong wooden structures designed to break up packed ice and to prevent it from damaging the bridges during the depths of winter. Plate 8 shows a collection of people standing and looking into the river at the position of the fourth support on Petrovskii Bridge. Note the hut in the left-hand corner of the picture at the far end of the bridge.

Figure 4: Petrovskii Bridge and Petrovskii and Krestovskii Islands

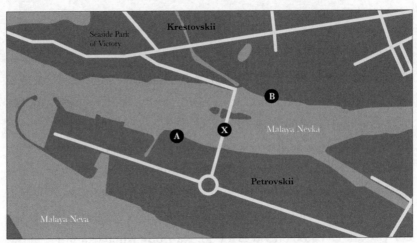

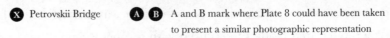

A substantial point of interest is that Vladimir Purishkevich states that the Malaya Nevka was identified as the place to dispose of the body on 13 December. If this is a diary entry and not a later manifestation of his recollection of events, then the conspirators had decided on a location where the river was not frozen over three days before they disposed of the body. I have seen how rapidly rivers freeze, and this does not sound realistic. Feliks Yusupov identifies the date as 26 November, and this is the date reported in *Rasputin: The Last Word* – nineteen-plus days before the body was disposed of. More sensibly Maurice Paléologue suggested that the reconnaissance was carried out the evening before by Sergei Sukhotin. There is no evidence that the conspirators carried ice-breaking equipment. One might wonder if Yusupov or his alleged companions actually decided on the site, or did someone else make the decision?

On 17 December at 2.00 p.m. some blood and a piece of cloth were found on the support and the buttress beneath the fourth section of Petrovskii Bridge. An overshoe, later identified as Rasputin's, was found on some ice between the bridge supports. Plate 9 shows the blood on the bridge support (circled). Note also the ladder between the bridge rail and the base of the support, which also appears in Plate 8.

Why is any of this relevant? Simply because Yusupov in his original memoirs and Paléologue suggest that the body was recovered 65 metres upstream from the bridge on the Krestovskii (north) shore. This is significant because if the body was recovered upstream, then whether the Malaya Nevka is tidal becomes a key issue. If the Nevka is not tidal and the flow is towards the Gulf of Finland, it would be impossible for Rasputin's body to float for 65 metres against the moderately strong currents of the river. If it was found 65 metres upstream, he could not have been thrown off Petrovskii Bridge. But it is clear that the forensic evidence supports the fact he was thrown off the bridge at the position of the fourth support, his body colliding with the support, and the position of the overshoe confirms this.

According to the archivists at the Royal Geographical Society, 'tidal influence in the Baltic Sea is imperceptible'.[1] I am grateful to them for supplying me with that information. It was therefore necessary to establish from where the photograph was taken as this would identify whether it was possible for the body to have been thrown off the bridge and come to rest at point A or point B in Figure 4. I compared photographs of the bridge now with those taken at the time, particularly any identifying features that might locate where the scene-of-crime photographs were taken. I am extremely grateful again for the assistance of Rudy De Casseres in the process of resolving this aspect of the investigation.

De Casseres identified the building in Plate 10 as a rest home for the Imperial Theatre Association, built in 1902 by B. A. Almedingen. It still operates, under the name of the Home for Veterans of the Stage, and is named after M. G. Savina, a leading Russian actress who co-founded the home. As this building is not shown in Plate 8, it is safe to assume that the photograph was taken from the Petrovskii Island bank of the Malaya Nevka looking towards Krestovskii Island.

The following police statements are to be found in the GARF Rasputin file:

On 17 December 1916 police officers of station No. 4 drafted the statement regarding the following: at 2 p.m. today policeman Kordukov, badge number 1876, stated that having assumed his duties at post No. 2, he received a report from the bridge guard Fyodor Kuz'min. Kuz'min stated that he was told by passing workers whose names he doesn't know that Petrovskii Bridge bears traces of blood; similar traces are also visible on the bridge supports. Having arrived at the location he in fact noticed the mentioned traces of blood. Following this report Police Inspector Asonov, Kordukov and Kuz'min arrived at the location, where they conducted an inspection in accordance with Article 258 of the Criminal Code, and established the following: traces of blood in the form of small drops were indeed visible on the decking of the fourth section of Petrovskii Bridge, and the wooden supports also bared minor traces of blood, again in the form of small drops. In the gap between the supports, 1.5 square arshins* in size, a man's

---

* 1 arshin = 28 inches (71 centimetres).

galosh, a warm brown size 10 shoe manufactured by Treigol'nik, was found. The bridge barrier also had traces of blood at a distance of 1.5 arshins. The search of the stretch of water opposite the location mentioned in the statement, which had not yet been covered in ice and where pools of water had formed, was conducted and did not reveal anything suspicious. The removed galosh has been handed to Kuz'min until further instructions are given. A corresponding record is made in this statement.

When questioned, the guard of Petrovskii Bridge, Fyodor Kuz'min . . . explained that he started his shift at the said bridge at 12 noon today and did not notice any blood when he did his round on the bridge. About an hour later he was on the opposite side of the bridge, namely on the side of Krestovskii Island, and some unknown workers who passed by told him that there were traces of blood next to the fourth section. When he arrived at the place referred to by the workers he actually noticed traces of blood on the decking, parapet and support and also a man's shoe on the bottom between the supports. He reported this to policeman Kordukov. The guard did not see the incident and can't provide any further comments.

Rasputin's overshoe or galosh was recovered by Kuz'min, according to the statements he and Kordukov gave to Colonel Popel' on 18 December under Article 23 of the Rules on Areas Declared Governed by Martial Law:

My name is Vasilii Fedorov Kordukov. I am thirty-six years of age, and of Christian religion. Title: peasant of Ivanovskoe village and volost, Bezhetskii District, Tverskaya Province. I serve as a policeman at the 4th Petrograd police station. I reside at 8 Petrovskii Avenue.

At 12 noon on 17 December I assumed my duty at the post on Petrovskii Avenue across from No. 8. Shortly after 1 p.m. the bridge guard Fyodor Kuz'min told me that he had found traces of blood on the panel/pavement and railings of the fourth section of Petrovskii Bridge. I went there straightaway and noticed blood also on one of the bridge's supports. There was a dark brown men's shoe on the ice between that support and the one next to it. I reported what I had seen to the 4th Petrograd police station and to the local police inspector Asonov, who then drafted a statement. At 2 p.m. Kuz'min picked up the shoe with a boat hook in the presence of Asonov and myself. The shoe was delivered to the police station.

My name is Fyodor Kuz'min. I am forty-eight years of age, and of Christian religion. Title: peasant of Lyanino village, Nikolo-Moshenskaya Volost, Borovichskii District, Novgorodskaya Province. I reside at Flat 11, 11/1 Petrovskii Avenue.

I started my shift at Petrovskii Bridge at 12 noon on 17 December. Around 2 p.m. I was approached by two workers unknown to me previously who reported that they had found traces of blood on the bridge. I followed them and saw that there were blood stains on the panel/pavement, on the squared timber of the railings and also on one of the bridge supports. Moreover, a dark brown galosh was on the ice next to the bridge support. Small blood drops, not stains, could be seen on the support. At 2 p.m. I picked up the galosh on inspector Asonov's orders and kept it till midnight, when it was requested by the 4th Petrograd police station. Point duty policeman Kordukov and me delivered the galosh to the department. The statement has been read.

The overshoe was identified as Rasputin's by his daughters, as we see from this statement by Police Inspector Mikhailov, dated 18 December:

The brown size 10 shoe manufactured by Treigol'nik found under Petrovskii Bridge on the river Nevka today at three o'clock has been presented to . . . Mariya and Varvara Rasputina-Novaya, residing at 64 Gorokhovaya Street. They confirmed that the shoe belonged to their father; it was the right size and looked the same. Moreover, two agents of the Secret Political Police Department, the door lady and a Mr Simanovich, who were at the apartment, confirmed that the shoe belonged to Rasputin-Novykh.

A search of the river by divers was ordered but the body was not found until 19 December and then by a river policeman walking on the ice who noticed a fur coat trapped beneath, approximately 65 metres from the bridge. The ice was cut open and Rasputin's frozen body discovered. The post mortem was held on the night of 20 December.

Forensics: bodies in water

I want now to deal with the issue of drowning and bodies immersed in water. My main reason is the myth that Rasputin was alive when he was thrown into the Nevka; he was not! Paléologue suggested in his memoirs that the myth of Rasputin being alive when he was thrown in the river was developed to prevent his canonisation, as under Russian Orthodox law a person who died by drowning could not be raised to the sainthood. I have checked with authorities within the Russian Orthodox diocese in Great Britain. They state that no such injunction exists or existed.

When I first saw photographs of Rasputin's body and started to read books on the subject, I had assumed that Rasputin had been placed through a fairly small hole in the ice. The photograph of the bridge from the State Archives shows a large expanse of water around the bridge that is clearly not frozen. Whether this is the product of ice clearance by police officers searching for the body or whether the gap occurred naturally is important. The initial search of the river proved negative, which I find strange in the extreme. As I stood on the bridge on the two days we filmed there I ran several experiments to gauge the river's flow. The Nevka is a moderate-flowing river running into the Gulf of Finland. As it passes under the bridge the flow tows towards the left bank. This is the Petrovskii Island side of the river. I watched several pieces of flotsam move down the river and noticed they quickly moved to the Petrovskii bank, ending their journey about 60 metres from the bridge.

However, we need to consider how cold the water would have been and the equipment available to police divers at the time. I have witnessed the recovery of bodies from the Thames and even today in large dark-water rivers it is done by touch. So it would have been in 1916. On 5 May 1882 a school for divers was founded at Kronshtadt, about 30 kilometres from St Petersburg, on the order of Tsar Alexander III. It was the first such school in the world and in those days it was regarded as an honour to be able to study there. Photographs of the period show the school trained 'hard hat' divers, wearing a heavy metal helmet, weighty boots and a thick waterproof suit. They would have been connected to an air pump, which itself would have been on a boat or the river bank. Imagine searching that dark, ice cold expanse of a river for a body. The divers' movement would have been limited in their heavy boots and cumbersome clothing.

We know the bridge span is 300 metres and the body was found 65 metres from the bridge. If the divers had searched this whole expanse of water they would have covered 19,500 square metres. Even narrowing the search to a line drawn from bridge support four they would have needed to search 3,250 square metres of river bottom. The chance of missing a body in such circumstances is extraordinarily high.

But I then stood in the position where the body was thrown over the barrier and threw several pieces of wood into the river. Not surprisingly they towed to the left in exactly the same way as the flotsam I had seen earlier. If I could conduct this schoolboy experiment, why could not investigators have traced the flow and likely direction of Rasputin's body in 1916? Driftwood thrown in to the left or right of the bridge support moved in largely parallel diagonal lines towards the left bank. This is of some importance when discussing the disposal of Rasputin's fur coat.

Had the body been thrown from the centre of the bridge or from the Krestovskii side, it would, in all probability, have floated out into the gulf. Repeated exercises with driftwood from the centre and Krestovskii side of the bridge confirmed this. My assessment is that the investigators and divers assumed the body had sunk and bumped along the river bed towards the Gulf of Finland.

I also need to explode the myth that in some way the body was carried from the bridge along the river bank and then deposited in the water through a hole in the ice, as suggested by Dr Lazovert. Firstly the flow of the river would have taken the body to almost exactly the position it was found in. The body, had it been carried by the murderers to a hole in the ice where Rasputin was found, would have to have been manhandled, wrapped in its shroud, for approximately 65 metres along what is even now an overgrown and undulating river bank; in the pitch black of night, this is not probable. Even less probable is that they would have then risked walking on the ice, carrying such a heavy burden, before placing the body into the 'prepared ice hole'.

During my research I found a very valuable paper on the website of the Centre for Forensic and Legal Medicine (formerly the Department of Forensic Medicine) at Dundee University.[2] The following sections of the paper are reported verbatim:

A body in water will usually sink but because the specific gravity of a body is very close to that of water then small variations, e.g. air trapped in clothing, have a considerable effect on buoyancy. Having sunk to the bottom the body will remain there until putrefactive gas formation decreases the specific gravity of the body and creates sufficient buoyancy to allow it to rise to the surface and float. Heavy clothing and weights attached to the body may delay but will not usually prevent the body rising. Putrefaction proceeds at a slower rate in water than in air, in sea water than in fresh water and in running water than in stagnant water. The principal determinant is the temperature of the water so that in deep very cold water, e.g. the North American Great Lakes or the ocean, the body may never resurface.

For the Thames, Simpson [a leading British pathologist] offers the following guidelines for the resurfacing times: June to August: 2 days; April, May, September and October: 3–5 days; November, December: 10–14 days; January, February; possibly no resurfacing. At water temperatures persistently below 45 degrees Fahrenheit [7 degrees Celsius] there may be no appreciable decomposition after several weeks.

In the water the body floats face down with the head lower than the rest of the body so that lividity is most prominent on the head, neck and anterior chest. Lividity is often blotchy and irregularly distributed, reflecting movement of the body in the water. It is not intensive and appears a pink or light red colour. In cold water it can be dusky and cyanotic. It may be difficult to recognise due to swelling with water of the upper layers of the skin with resultant loss of translucency.

. . . The body cools in water about twice as fast as in air and reaches the temperature of the water usually within five to six hours and nearly always within twelve hours.

It has to be accepted that there are many variables in establishing time of death from a body's temperature. In this case it is hardly relevant as Rasputin was 'deep frozen', having been in the ice-cold water of the Nevka for over forty-eight hours. We know from the evidence that the ice was thick enough for a river policeman to stand on it.

Lividity, as mentioned in the Dundee paper, is the process by which blood stops circulating after the heart has stopped beating. What normally happens at this point is that the blood supply, or at least any blood that remains within the corpse depending on the nature of the person's death, will settle in direct response to gravity. For example an individual found lying on their stomach would be found with all the blood from their back heading towards the ground. Lividity also displays itself as a dark purple discolouration of the body and can be referred to as livor mortis or post mortem hypostasis. Any part of the body which has come into contact with a firm surface for a period of time, such as a floor or bench top, will show signs of this during lividity: this impression against the skin displays itself as an indentation surrounded by gravity-pulled blood.

Lividity begins to work through the deceased within thirty minutes of their heart stopping and can take up to twelve hours. It can be altered by moving the body during the first six hours of death, but after this period it becomes fixed as blood vessels begin to break down within the body. The rate of this process will become relevant when we discuss the timings of the events surrounding the disposal of Rasputin's body.

It is also relevant to note that the University of Dundee paper identifies that

> buffeting in the water commonly produces post-mortem head injuries, which may be difficult to distinguish from injuries sustained during life. The presence of bleeding usually distinguishes ante-mortem from post-mortem injuries. However, the head-down position of a floating corpse causes passive congestion of the head with blood, so that post-mortem injuries tend to bleed, creating the diagnostic confusion.

*

Despite analysing the times that the various witnesses say shots were fired it seems difficult to reconcile them with the comments that both Yusupov and Purishkevich make about having to hurry to remove the body as 'dawn was approaching' (see Table 1). Where times are included in statements or accounts I have shown them against the witness who gives that time. Purishkevich's time for the basement shooting is calculated from taking his initial timing of 12.45 a.m. and then adding the various intervals he refers to. He is specific about the yard shooting time and backtracking half an hour from 3.00, as he says it was half an hour since he had seen Rasputin on the floor, we come to the same figure.

Purishkevich tells us that Lazovert, Sukhotin and Dmitrii were to drive from the Yusupov Palace to the Warsaw station, where Mrs Purishkevich and Mrs Lazovert were to burn Rasputin's clothes. Then Lazovert and his passengers would load the car onto the supply wagon connected to Purishkevich's train. They would then all go by taxi or on foot to the Belosel'skii-Belozerskii Palace (which had belonged to Dmitrii since 1910) on Nevskii Avenue, where they would collect Dmitrii's car. Of course, according to Lazovert, he was there when Rasputin attempted to escape.

Purishkevich tells us that Dmitrii drove his car fairly slowly through the city to the Nevka: 'It was very late and the grand duke evidently feared that great speed would attract the suspicion of the police.' I have then used his timings and added a little for Dmitrii's return. This would allow one and half hours for travelling to the Warsaw station, trying to dispose of Rasputin's coat, loading the car onto the train, then driving to the Belosel'skii-Belozerskii Palace to pick up Dmitrii's car and returning to the Yusupov Palace to pick up the body (see Table 1).

Table 1: Witnesses' accounts of timing

Witness	Shots heard	Yard incident	Dmitrii returns	Travel to bridge	Final time
Bobkov	3.00 a.m.			30 mins	
Lazukov	3.00 a.m.			30 mins	
Yefimov	2.30 a.m.			30 mins	
Vlasyuk	4.00 a.m.			30 mins	
Yusupov	2.30 a.m.+			30 mins	
Purishkevich	2.30 a.m.	3.00 a.m.	+30 mins (estimated)	30 mins	4.00 a.m.

As a result of my initial analysis based on Purishkevich's evidence I decided to conduct a more detailed examination of the timings and I am very grateful to Gerald Brooke and colleagues for checking distances to and from various locations for me. By car, based on 1916-type speeds, the timings work out as follows:

- Yusupov Palace to Warsaw station: 15 minutes
- Warsaw Station to Belosel'skii-Belozerskii Palace: 25 minutes (To walk as suggested by Purishkevich as an option: 50 minutes)
- Belosel'skii-Belozerskii Palace to Yusupov Palace: 10 minutes
- Yusupov Palace to Petrovskii Bridge: 30 minutes
- Petrovskii Bridge to Belosel'skii-Belozerskii Palace: 30 minutes-plus
- Cab to Warsaw station from Belosel'skii-Belozerskii Palace: 25 minutes

This in fact is an over-generous estimate as Purishkevich tells us that he and Lazovert returned to where Dmitrii was staying, caught a cab, and 'already by 5.00 paid the cabbie on the bridge by the Warsaw station'. If his timings are correct then, allowing for the story that Dmitrii's car broke down a number of times between Petrovskii Bridge and the Belosel'skii-Belozerskii Palace, the last time near the Peter and Paul Fortress, the body would have been disposed of by 3.30 hours at the latest and probably by 3.00.

The story of dawn approaching is another red herring. The murder occurred close to the winter solstice; dawn in Petrograd would have been a long way off even at 6.00 a.m. In fact the sun set at about 4.45 p.m. on 16 December 1916 and rose at 10.05 a.m. the next day, so nowhere near the times that Purishkevich recalls that 'dawn was approaching'. We know from Constable Vlasyuk's evidence that Yusupov left the palace at about 5.00. We need to recall that Yefimov tells us that the only time he saw a car on Moika Embankment after hearing the shots was at about 3.30–4.00, travelling from the Blue Bridge. The car did not stop; Lazukov tells us that there were no cars in the yard of 92 Moika Embankment at the time he heard the 'shots'.

However, the real timings, as calculated above from Purishkevich's timings, would mean the following sequence:

- 2.30: Rasputin shot, all assemble in basement dining room, look at the body, chat, go upstairs, take fur coat, boots etc., then put on their own coats and get into Purishkevich's car, presumably unloading weights and chains mentioned in Yusupov and Purishkevich's accounts – see below (30 minutes).
- 3.00: Drive to Warsaw station (15 minutes), park, board train, try to burn clothes and load Purishkevich's car onto train (30 minutes minimum).
- 3.45: Take cab to Belosel'skii-Belozerskii Palace (25 minutes).
- 4.10: Get into Dmitrii's car, load fur coat etc. and drive to Yusupov Palace (10 minutes, plus, say, 10 minutes for transferring to Dmitrii's car).
- 4.30: Arrive at Yusupov Palace, explanation about what has occurred, transfer weights and chains to Dmitrii's car. Bring body up from basement and load into car (say 20 minutes minimum).
- 4.50: Dmitrii drives slowly to Petrovskii Bridge (30 minutes minimum). Disposal of body, coat, weights etc. (say 10 minutes minimum).
- 5.30: Drive to Belosel'skii-Belozerskii Palace. Dmitrii's car keeps breaking down and is repaired by Lazovert (30 minutes plus 15 minutes minimum for breakdown).
- 6.15: Find overshoe in Dmitrii's car, say goodbyes, call cab and return to Warsaw station (35 minutes minimum).

By now the time is 6.50, nearly two hours after Purishkevich says he and Lazovert returned to the train.

If we were to take the timing of the 'not very loud' shots from Lazukov and Bobkov, who say they went off around 3.00, it would be 7.20 before Purishkevich and Lazovert returned to the Warsaw station. The fact is the sequence of events and journeys as described did not take place.

We need to re-examine Purishkevich's evidence in respect of the body's disposal:

These were my recollections as I sat in the rear of the car, with the lifeless corpse of the 'venerable old man', which we were taking to its eternal resting place, lying at my feet. I looked out of the window. To judge by the surrounding houses and the endless fences, we had already left the city. There were very few lights. The road deteriorated and we hit bumps and holes which made the body lying at our feet bounce around (despite the soldier sitting on it). I felt a nervous tremor run through me at each bump as my knees touched the repulsive, soft corpse which, despite the cold, had not yet completely stiffened. At last the bridge from which we were to fling Rasputin's body into the hole in the ice appeared in the distance. Dmitrii Pavlovich slowed down, drove onto the left side of the bridge and stopped by the guard rail.

Purishkevich describes how the car's headlight beams briefly swept across a sentry-box on the other side of the bridge to the right. Dmitrii turned the lights off, whereupon all was plunged into darkness, but he kept the engine running. Purishkevich continues:

I opened the car doors quietly and, as quickly as possible, jumped out and went over to the railing. The soldier and Dr Lazovert followed me and then Lieutenant S., who had been sitting by the grand duke, joined us and together we swung Rasputin's corpse and flung it forcefully into the ice hole just by the bridge. (Dmitrii Pavlovich stood guard in front of the car.) Since we had forgotten to fasten the weights on the corpse with a chain, we hastily threw these, one after another, after it. Likewise, we stuffed the chains into the dead man's coat and threw it into the same hole. Next, Dr Lazovert searched in the dark car and found one of Rasputin's boots, which he also flung off the bridge. All of this took no more than two or three minutes. Then Dr Lazovert, Lieutenant S. and the soldier got into the back of the car, and I got in next to Dmitrii Pavlovich. We turned on the headlights again and crossed the bridge.

How we failed to be noticed on the bridge is still amazing to me to this day. For, as we passed the sentry-box, we noticed a guard next to it. But he was sleeping so deeply that he had apparently not woken up even when . . . we had inadvertently not only lit up his sentry-box, but had even turned the lights on him.

Once across the bridge, Purishkevich says, the grand duke increased his speed, but there was something wrong with his car, as it broke down several times. Each time this happened, Lazovert jumped out, fiddled with the spark plugs and cleaned them, which managed to get the car going again. The last breakdown and repair occurred on Kamennoostrovskii Avenue, nearly opposite the Peter and Paul Fortress.

After cleaning [the plugs] there, we went faster, and arrived successfully at the palace of Sergei Aleksandrovich [the Belosel'skii-Belozerskii Palace] where Dmitrii Pavlovich was staying. On the way back . . . I said to him: 'You know, Dmitrii Pavlovich, I think that our big mistake was in throwing the corpse into the water instead of leaving it somewhere conspicuous. It is possible that a false Rasputin might appear, since this craft is a rather profitable one.'

'Maybe you are right,' the grand duke replied, 'but what is done cannot be undone.'

Just as we arrived at the palace gates and were getting out of the car, we saw, to our great amazement, Rasputin's second boot, which

137

we had overlooked. At the same time, we saw spots of blood which had trickled from the dead man onto the carpet of the car. The grand duke instructed his servant, who had met us on the steps and who struck me as having been initiated into the whole affair, to burn the carpeting and Rasputin's boot.

Lazovert does not help us significantly: 'We bundled him up in a sheet and carried him to the river's edge. Ice had formed, but we broke it and threw him in.'

We know from the positioning of the blood stains and the recovery of his galosh that Rasputin's body entered the river Nevka at the fourth support along the bridge from Petrovskii Island. Blood on the bridge and the bridge rail, together with blood and other debris on the support, show conclusively that this is where his body was hauled into the river. It is the considered view of Professor Vladimir Zharov and his two colleagues that Rasputin's hitting the bridge support may account for some of his severe facial injuries.

Purishkevich explained how they 'flung the body forcefully' into the river, after swinging it back and forth. He, Dmitrii, Lazovert and 'a soldier' forgot to tie the weighted chains to Rasputin's body. This is rather strange given that the two pood weights were of a considerable size (a pood is an ancient Russian measure of weight equivalent to 16.4 kilograms or 36 pounds 2 ounces) and that Purishkevich says that they were squeezed into the back of the car. So the body went in, didn't sink and was caught in the current, which took it approximately 60 metres at an angle of about 40 degrees from the bridge support towards Petrovskii Island. Then they allegedly realised they had forgotten to throw his fur coat into the river, as well as an overboot, so they threw them into the same hole. Purishkevich claimed that the coat was weighted down by the weights and chains they had forgotten to attach to Rasputin's body.

Miraculously, when the body was found, the fur coat had wrapped itself around Rasputin; how could this have happened? The fact is that for the fur coat to have even been close to Rasputin's body it would have had to be thrown into the river in exactly the same spot as the body and without the chains. The coat could not have wrapped itself around Rasputin and as it was meant to have been weighted it would have landed up in a different place from the body. Rasputin was thrown into the river wrapped in his coat.

Given all the fuss that the conspirators made about disposing of the coat, by taking it to Purishkevich's train to burn it, were they likely to forget to throw it in the river? They even say they found another galosh in Dmitrii's car when they arrived at the Belosel'skii-Belozerskii Palace – very careless! Given Purishkevich's obviously flawed recollection of the events at the bridge I would suggest that he was not there. Someone else disposed of the body.

I now want to deal with one of the 'fantasy' arguments around Rasputin's death: that the position of his arms and his clenched fists indicate that he was alive when he was thrown in the river and attempted to free himself from his bonds. I have considered this carefully and reflected on the evidence provided by Professor Zharov. The post mortem revealed no evidence of death by drowning, and Zharov supports this.

When I first looked at the post mortem photographs in detail I postulated two hypotheses: firstly, that rigor mortis had set in before the body was thrown into the Nevka; secondly, that the corpse reflected the position of the body as it floated in the river, rigor mortis setting in some time later.

For the first option to be realistic rigor mortis would have set in within a maximum of $1\frac{1}{2}$ hours, if my calculations of the time the shots were first heard are correct (a consensus time is 2.30 a.m., with disposal of the body by 4.00 at the latest). This is well outside the rule of thumb, admittedly very unpredictable, that rigor commences within six hours, takes another six hours to become fully established, remains for twelve hours and passes off during the succeeding twelve hours.

The Dundee University website usefully highlights research conducted by P. F. Niderkorn in 1872 that observed the onset of rigor in 113 bodies.[3] In only two of the observations was rigor complete in two hours; it was complete within three hours in fourteen cases and within four hours in thirty-one. The site goes on to say that if the temperature is below 10 degrees Celsius it is exceptional for rigor mortis to develop, but if the environmental temperature is then raised, rigor mortis is said to develop in the normal manner. Interestingly, the joints of the fingers and toes often become markedly flexed during the development of rigor. This could account for the positions of Rasputin's fingers in the photographs.

My thoughts then focused on a passage in *Nicholas and Alexandra: The Last Imperial Family* where Grand Duke Nikolai Mikhailovich suggests that Rasputin had been sitting down when Yusupov shot him.[4] Visualise the scene: a drunken Rasputin sprawled across the dining room table, his head on the table top and his arms out in front, also supported by the table. We know from Edvard Radzinskii's research into the Rasputin files that Rasputin had previously been observed by police in a similar position when in a drunken stupor on board a boat. Under this scenario you would have the first shot to Rasputin's left side, the second shot to the back, and the fatal shot, across the table, to the forehead. I rehearsed this position several times with family members. It allows the shot to the left side, and the right-side-of-the-back shot is also feasible, as is the shot to the forehead. The 'dead' family members ended up in a position extremely close to the shape of Rasputin's body on top of the Nevka's ice.

The body was left in the room, by the log fire, while the conspirators celebrated upstairs. We know the room was warm because Rasputin had taken his coat off and was dressed in his shirt and trousers. The heat from the fire could have induced earlier rigor mortis if he was close enough to it. The conspirators came back down to wrap and dispose of the corpse; rigor mortis had started or was in place. The body was wrapped in cloth and in Rasputin's fur coat, bound and placed in the car. It would have been inconvenient to say the least to wrap the body in the position described above, load it in the car and then convey it to the bridge. If Rasputin was about 5 feet 9 inches (175 centimetres) tall then they would have needed a large car to take such a stiff body with the arms extended.

There is a condition known as cadaveric spasm that is a form of muscular stiffening which occurs at the moment of death and which persists into the period of rigor mortis. Its cause is unknown but it is usually associated with violent deaths in circumstances of intense emotion. It has medico-legal importance because it records the last act of life. It can affect all muscles but most frequently involves groups of muscles only, such as those of the forearms and hands. Rasputin's death was violent and emotional so cadaveric spasm could well have occurred.

Interestingly, Purishkevich helps us when he says:

> The road deteriorated and we hit bumps and holes [it was no different in 2004] which made the body lying at our feet bounce around (despite the soldier sitting on it). I felt a nervous tremor run through me at each bump as my knees touched the repulsive, soft corpse which, despite the cold, had not yet completely stiffened.

Or does he help us? The body was allegedly wrapped; how would he know it had not fully stiffened?

I again knew I had missed something in the photographs of Rasputin on the Nevka ice but I couldn't pick up the clues I needed. It was Professor Zharov's reconsideration of the Kosorotov post mortem that allowed me to see what I had missed. Zharov says:

> On the 'key photo', one can see that the body (the beard is clearly visible) is lying on its back, face up. The arms are raised to shoulder level and the elbows are bent; the hands are lying at the level of the head at some distance from each other. The right hand is higher than the left one. The fingers of the right hand are bent, the nails of the fingers rest on the surface of the thumb. The fingers of the left hand are in similar position, but they are more clenched. Around the right wrist there is a loop of a rope, there is a knot with several ends on the forearm. On the left wrist one could not see a rope. There is a white shirt on the body. It is pleated on the chest and the lower end of the shirt is level with the middle of the chest. Underneath this shirt there is an undershirt. Its hem is tucked into the trousers in the front, but at the back it is not tucked in, and is rolled up as high as the middle of the spine. The lower part of the body is wrapped up in a dark cloth. There is an indentation in the cloth in the region of the shins, suggesting that this part of the body is tied up. Between the waist and the feet one could see about seven coils of the rope. The knees are bent.

Plate 11 gives a general view of the body and, rather closer to the camera, what is considered to be Rasputin's fur coat. Next to the body, on the upper left side, there is a bundle of what appears to be the same material as is wrapped around Rasputin's legs. On closer examination it can clearly be seen that this is so. So it appears reasonable to assume the whole body was wrapped in this material and it was tied around the body as the legs are bound with rope. Plate 12 shows clearly the blood staining on the right-hand side of the body and the rope tied around the legs.

Zharov provides more information:

A river policeman happened to be cutting the ice on the river and noticed the sleeve of a beaver fur coat frozen to the ice. The police cut the ice near it and in fifteen minutes discovered the body of Rasputin.

. . . The head was cracked in several places. Tufts of hair were missing (probably because the body fell from the bridge head first onto the hard ice), the beard was frozen to the clothes, the chest and the face were bruised and so was one eye. His feet and hands were tied tightly with a rope; the right hand was clenched into a fist. The body was wrapped up in a beaver fur coat, one sleeve of which was missing.

So we have a body wrapped firstly in cloth and tied up, and then around the torso is placed a fur coat. It is important to note that when found his feet and hands were bound tightly with rope. So my hypothesis is that Rasputin was wrapped in the cloth, which was bound up with ropes. The arms, which were used to carry or drag the body, were not bound into this 'mummification'. Purishkevich confirms this mummification: 'I ordered the soldiers to hurry and find some cloth from somewhere and to wrap the corpse tightly from head to foot and then bind the swaddled thing with cord.'

The fur coat was put on Rasputin as he would normally wear it. The hands, we are told, on recovery from the Nevka were bound. We are also told that one arm was missing from the fur coat. It is possible that this arm came away as the body was tipped over the bridge parapet into the Nevka. It appears that the cloth covering the top of the body was removed by the police, as was the fur coat.

In modern times the body would initially be photographed in the water, if possible through the ice; the sleeve of the fur coat was visible to the river policeman, so the ice was not entirely opaque. The body, once revealed by the process of cutting the ice, would be photographed where it lay, and the whole process would also be videoed. Once removed and placed on a sledge or boards it would be photographed still wrapped in the fur coat and cloth. Bonds would not be cut before it was photographed. In a case such as this it is probable that the pathologist and forensic scientists would be called to the scene to supervise the removal and initial examination of the body. Unfortunately the photographs that today we would expect as a matter of routine appear not to have been taken in December 1916, although this may be an unfair comment, as other photographs may have been taken that no longer survive. Fortunately Plate 13, showing Rasputin next to the 'ice hole', also shows a length of rope hanging down from the right wrist which has been cut.

The body was removed from the water and had some of the covering removed, in all probability before the photographer arrived. I can understand why the clothing was removed and bonds cut; this would be to allow identification of the body. But had Professor Kosorotov viewed the body in situ, what other evidence might have been available to us and, more importantly, the Russian detectives in December 1916? It is probable that forensic evidence was lost at the point of recovery.

Lifting a dead body unsurprisingly is like lifting a 'dead' weight. In the mid-1970s I was involved in the investigation of the murder of a teenage girl who had been found in the back garden of a house, abutting a communal alleyway. It was suggested that the body had been thrown over the garden fence that was about 5 feet (150 centimetres) high. I doubted that this was possible. At the time I was heavily involved in judo and the British team had just purchased a leather-covered training dummy, which resembled a human being and weighed about the same as the victim. I brought the dummy to the scene and tried (I was pretty fit and strong at the time) to throw it in a number of ways over the fence. I couldn't. Later on we established that the girl had access to the garden and had gone there willingly.

Lifting Rasputin's body over the parapet on Petrovskii Bridge, which is at about lower chest height for me, would have taken considerable effort. There are a number of ways the body could have been thrown into the river. First it could have been propped up against the parapet and then tipped over the edge onto the supports below. Purishkevich suggests it was swung and then flung over the bridge, but neither he nor Lazovert were in the first flush of youth and Purishkevich does not look in the least fit, so throwing the body over the bridge would have been an effort. The thought of the four men each trying to grab a part of Rasputin's body to swing it over the bridge is somewhat laughable and I believe that the body was propped up against the railings and tipped over head first.

The journey from Petrovskii Bridge to Dmitrii's palace was strange, to say the least. The conspirators had concerns when they drove onto the bridge about alerting the sentry on the far side, yet we are told that Dmitrii drove past the sentry on the way home. Why? The position on the bridge where the body was thrown into the Nevka is less than a quarter of the way across. Dmitrii could have avoided alerting the sentry by reversing off the bridge and retracing his journey from Moika Embankment. He did not take this option and instead drove across the bridge onto Krestovskii Island. Incidentally, Radzinskii talks about Dmitrii and his companions 'retracing their route' from Petrovskii Bridge, but this must be another factual error if Purishkevich's account is what happened. Purishkevich tells us that

145

the car broke down on a number of occasions, the final time on Kamennoostrovskii Avenue. From his account it would appear that they drove straight to Dmitrii's residence on Nevskii Avenue.

To travel to the Warsaw station from the Yusupov Palace, they would have turned right down Moika Embankment and then right again into Voznesenskii Avenue, which leads straight to the station at Obvodnyi Kanal Embankment. The journey to Dmitrii's palace at 41 Nevskii Avenue, on the Fontanka, would probably be via Voznesenskii Avenue right onto Reka Fontanka Embankment and then to Dmitrii's home at the junction of Nevskii Avenue.

To get to Petrovskii Bridge from 92 Moika Embankment the conspirators would likely have taken this route: Nikolaevskii Bridge, Universitetskaya Embankment, Tuchkov Bridge, Zhdanovskaya Street, Petrovskii Avenue, Petrovskii Bridge. Or they could have gone via Dvortsovyi Bridge, Birzhevaya Square, Birzhevoi Bridge, Aleksandrovskii Avenue then as above. The probable route back to Dmitrii's on Nevskii Avenue is as follows: Petrovskii Bridge, Krestovskii Avenue, Malo-Krestovskii Bridge, Krestovskaya Embankment, Zapadnaya Street, Berezovaya Lane, Kamennoostrovskii Avenue, Troitskii Bridge, Milionnaya Street, Nevskii Avenue.

CHAPTER EIGHT

FORENSICS PROVE THE LIE

The bullet wounds all look like close range shots, which are
consistent with less than 20 centimetres (8 inches).

Martin Parker, lead forensic scientist, National Ballistics Intelligence Service,
January 2010

Kosorotov's original post mortem and additional forensic evidence

I open with the details of the original post mortem, the findings of
which have been consistently ignored over the years as the fairy tale
'accepted' version of the murder has been told and retold. Whether
these details are a complete or an exact record is a matter of great
controversy; however, much of what is reported is supported by the
scene-of-crime photographs from Petrovskiï Bridge, the post mortem
and the expert re-examination by Professor Vladimir Zharov and
his colleagues. Professor Kosorotov was clear that the three bullet
wounds were fired at close range and by different-calibre weapons.
The forensic evidence exposes the lies and the myths of Yusupov's
and Purishkevich's tale. However, he and other forensic scientists can
tell us much more.

147

I, Professor Kosorotov, declare that I have been to the autopsy of Rasputin's dead body, on 20 December 1916 at ten o'clock in the evening, in the mortuary room of Chesmenskii Hospice. The body was recognised by his two daughters, his niece, his secretary and various witnesses.

We are told the post mortem lasted until 1 a.m.

The body is that of a man of about fifty years old, of medium size, dressed in a blue embroidered hospital robe, which covers a white shirt. His legs, in tall animal skin boots, are tied with a rope, and the same rope ties his wrists. His dishevelled hair is light brown, as are his long moustache and beard, and it's soaked with blood. His mouth is half open, his teeth clenched. His face below his forehead is covered in blood. His shirt too is also marked with blood. [All this can be confirmed factually by reference to the scene-of-crime photographs and post mortem photographs.] There are three bullet wounds. The first has penetrated the left side of the chest and has gone through the stomach and the liver. [This wound is shown clearly in Plate 14.]

Plate 15 is a control photograph from the University of Utah firearms tutorial.[1] It shows the 'sooting' around the wound that is evidence of a weapon fired from close range. Where the gun is held against the skin the outline of the muzzle may be found, which is known as a 'standsmark'.

Kosorotov continues: 'The second [bullet] has entered into the right side of the back and gone through the kidney.' (See Plate 16.) This is a similar wound to the one on the left side and is also caused by a firearm being fired at close range. 'The third has hit the victim on the forehead and penetrated into his brain.' (See Plate 17.)

Plate 18 is also from the University of Utah firearms tutorial. The starring effect is evident on this picture. Close examination of Plate 17 shows a similar, albeit less distinct, pattern on Rasputin's forehead. This indicates that the wound was caused by the weapon being fired at close range.

There are no pictures of the rear of Rasputin's head, probably because of the massive injuries that may have been caused. I believe that the photograph of Rasputin's upper body and head shows considerable matting and blood-soaked hair, and, as we have seen, Kosorotov describes his hair as 'soaked with blood', which I believe confirms my view. It has been suggested by several commentators that the absence of a photograph of the rear of his head proves that he was not shot at close range. However, Zharov usefully tells us: 'The huge wound on the head was too upsetting for the professor.' From examination of the pictures it can be seen that none of the other injuries to his head appear so grievous that they would 'upset' a professor of forensic medicine. The length of Rasputin's hair means that the exit wound, which in my belief would have been substantial, would have been covered over. Had Rasputin's head been wrapped in the blue material found around his body at the time the contact wound to the head was fired, the bullet would have probably caused massive damage to the brain and created a sizeable exit wound. The force of the bullet may have passed through the cloth, drawing with it a substantial amount of brain matter, blood and skull fragments.

Kosorotov concludes that the first two bullets hit Rasputin while he was standing, the third bullet hit him on the ground, and all three bullets came from different-calibre revolvers. Returning to the post mortem, he continues:

Examination of the head: the cerebral matter gave off a strong smell of alcohol. [This, as he refers to 'matter', might imply that the brain was considerably damaged by the close contact wound to the forehead.] Examination of the stomach: the stomach contains about twenty soup spoons of liquid smelling of alcohol. The examination reveals no trace of poison. Wounds: his left side has a weeping wound, due to some sort of slicing object or a sword. His right eye has come out of its cavity and falls down onto his face. At the corner of the right eye the membrane is torn. His right ear is hanging down and torn. His neck has a wound from some sort of rope tie. The victim's face and body carry traces of blows given by a supple but hard object. His genitals have been crushed by the action of a similar object.

He states the causes of death as follows:

Haemorrhage caused by the wound to the liver and the wound to the right kidney must have started the rapid decline of his strength. In this case, he would have died in ten or twenty minutes. At the moment of death the deceased was in a state of drunkenness. The first bullet passed through the stomach and the liver. This mortal blow had been shot from a distance of 20 centimetres. The wound on the right side, made at nearly exactly the same time as the first, was also mortal; it passed through the right kidney. The victim, at the time of the murder, was standing. When he was shot in the forehead, his body was already on the ground.

How did Kosorotov reach the conclusion that shots one and two were fired while Rasputin was standing, but that shot three was fired when he was lying down? I am not certain of the answer for the first two shots. In respect of the third it could be from debris attached to the blood-soaked and matted hair at the back of his head on the basis of a 'shored' exit wound. This is explained as follows: a shored exit wound occurs where the wound edges are abraded against an overlying object pressed firmly against the skin as the skin is pushed out from the body by the bullet. This may occur, for example when the victim is lying on the pavement when shot, or leaning against a wall, or even when the exit wound passes through a trouser belt. One study showed that such wounds have a greater wound diameter and demonstrate greater marginal abrasion than control wounds produced by the same weapons. However, Martin Parker, lead forensic scientist at the United Kingdom's National Ballistics Intelligence Service, who reviewed the post mortem photographs for me, concluded: 'The bullet wounds all look like close range shots, which are consistent with less than 20 centimetres [8 inches].' He also admitted that he could not understand, based on the post mortem alone, how Kosorotov could say that Rasputin was standing when hit by the first two bullets and lying down when shot in the forehead. He has in the past been able to identify victims who had been shot while lying down but this was based on the bullet passing through the body and being found in the ground underneath. Neither could he see how Kosorotov could determine the sequence of the shots.

Russia's leading forensic scientists review the original post mortem

This re-examination was carried out between 18 and 30 June 1993 by Vladimir Zharov, Igor' Panov and Valerii Vasil'yevskii. At the time Zharov was head of the Forensic Medical Analysis Bureau, and Panov and Vasil'yevskii were his deputies. Zharov and Panov both had a PhD in medicine and all three were supremely highly qualified.

They were all specialists in forensic medicine and between them had amassed eighty-five years' experience in the field.

They studied the documentary evidence relating to Rasputin's death together with various photographs with the purpose of providing an expert forensic analysis of the physical injuries and cause of death as described in the memoirs of Yusupov and Purishkevich. They repeat much of the detail contained in both conspirators' accounts.

Zharov reports:

A river policeman happened to be cutting the ice on the river and noticed the sleeve of a beaver fur coat frozen to the ice. The police cut the ice near it and in fifteen minutes discovered the body of Rasputin.

. . . The head was cracked in several places. Tufts of hair were missing (probably due to the fact that the body fell from the bridge head first onto the hard ice), the beard was frozen to the clothes, the chest and the face were bruised and so was one eye. His feet and hands were tied tightly with a rope; the right hand was clenched into a fist. The body was wrapped up in a beaver fur coat, one sleeve of which was missing.

The body was taken into a shed on the river bank. The ropes which bound the hands and feet, the fur coat and some other things were taken to be used as evidence.

The body was taken to Chesmenskii Hospice for autopsy. The autopsy was carried out by the professor of forensic medicine from the Military Medical Academy, D. P. Kosorotov, with the help of several police doctors. The autopsy lasted till 1 a.m.

The body was examined thoroughly for two hours. Apart from three gunshot wounds there were a lot of bruises. There was a lot of thick brown liquid in the stomach, but it was impossible to analyse it, because the autopsy was stopped on the orders of the Empress Alexandra Fyodorovna.

The autopsy showed up numerous injuries to the body, many of which Rasputin suffered posthumously. The entire right part of his head was smashed as a result of him being thrown off the bridge. Death was caused by an internal haemorrhage as a result of a gunshot wound in his stomach. He was shot at close range, according to Kosorotov, from left to right, through the stomach into the liver, the left part of which was shattered. There was another gunshot wound on the back, in the region of the spine, and the right kidney was shattered. One more gunshot was fired into the forehead from close range, most likely when the victim was already dead or dying. The chest wounds were clean cut, not messy, and were examined superficially. No signs of drowning were found: there was no water in the respiratory organs, the lungs were not swollen. Rasputin was thrown into the water when he was already dead.

The autopsy was carried out in very poor conditions. The source of light was oil lamps. In order to examine the insides of the chest and stomach an oil lamp had to be brought into the cavity. The huge wound on the head was too upsetting for the professor. He was surprised how much they were rushed by the authorities to finish the autopsy. He wanted to be thorough and methodical.

. . . Rasputin was a robust man of about 45 years. In the opinion of the medics carrying out the autopsy he could have lived another 45. He was drunk at the moment of his death. There was a strong smell of whisky on his breath. His brain was of normal size; there were no pathological signs of any sort in it.

In March 1917 the preliminary investigation of Rasputin's murder was closed, and its materials were allegedly destroyed.

An essential part of Zharov's re-examination was to establish that the body was in fact that of Rasputin. With his colleagues he viewed numerous photographs of Rasputin when alive and the scene-of-crime photographs and they confirmed that the body was indeed that of Rasputin.

The photographs of the crime scene are general and 'orientational' photos of different parts of the crime scene. They show from two different angles and in different sizes images of part of the wall of a three-storey house, part of the courtyard and the railing. In the wall of the house there is a closed door. The railing consists of seven segments; then we see the closed gates and then another four segments of the railing.

The snow in front of the door and in the courtyard had been cleared away and stored along the railing. If we assume that the door is 2.0–2.2 metres high then the distance from it to the distant open gate is 15–20 metres.

On one of the shots there is a dotted line. It starts on the threshold of the door and goes to the railing, at an angle of 40–45 degrees. It reaches a small snowdrift and then continues as a concave/convex line of approximately 10 metres. Then it bends at nearly 90 degrees towards the gate which is nearest to the house, and then, before it actually gets to that gate, it bends again, at a right angle, and continues along the railing, gradually disappearing. The dotted line seems to have been created artificially, so as to stand out on the snow. It consists of short dashes, with the same distance between them. There are 68–70 such dashes.

Zharov and his colleagues then consider the photographs of Petrovskii Bridge and the river:

There is a photo of Petrovskii Bridge with some people on it. In one of the photos there is a bridge pylon, on which blood was discovered in three places. Unfortunately, there is no scale. If we assume that the height of the people on the bridge is 1.6–1.7 metres then the distance from the railing of the bridge to the pylon on which the blood was discovered is approximately 4 metres. The blood stains on the pylon are encircled with a dotted line. Only in one place could one clearly see that the stains have an irregular rectangular or oval shape of 20 × 25 × 10 centimetres and an irregular triangular shape of 10 × 10 centimetres. Our attention was drawn to the fact that the blood stains on the upper beam of the pylon are exactly above the stains on the lower beam.

[Turning to the] photographs of the part of the river with pieces of ice of different sizes and an ice hole: near the edge of the ice hole there are ten or eleven boards with the body of a man lying between them. Closer to the shore, at some distance from the feet of the body, there is a dark object. It is shorter than the body. The object is covered with ice; it resembles in its shape a fur coat.

On [one photograph], one can see that the body (the beard is clearly visible) is lying on its back, face up. The arms are raised to shoulder level and the elbows are bent. The hands are lying at the level of the head at some distance from each other. The right hand is higher than the left one. The fingers of the right hand are bent, the nails of the fingers resting on the surface of the thumb. The fingers of the left hand are in a similar position, but they are more clenched. Around the right wrist there is a loop of a rope, and there is a knot with several ends on the forearm. On the left wrist one could not see a rope. There is a white shirt on the body. It is pleated on the chest and the lower end of the shirt is level with the middle of the chest. Underneath this shirt there is an undershirt. Its hem is tucked into the trousers at the front, but at the back it is not tucked in, and is rolled up as high as the middle of the spine. The lower part of the body is wrapped up in a dark cloth. There is an indentation in the cloth in the region of the shins, suggesting that this part of the body is tied up. Between the waist and the feet one could see about seven coils of the rope. The knees are bent.

Another photograph shows the head and the upper part of the body. The eyelids of the right eye are open unnaturally wide although, because of the wrong angle [from which the photograph was taken] and because of some mud and ice, we could not give our opinion on this.

In respect of the post mortem photographs they say:

This group have much better images; the body was washed and, as a result, the injuries are more visible.

On the back of the body there are some putrid spots and also some light-coloured spots caused by the pressure of the clothing on the body. There is a putrid venous web . . . In the middle of the forehead and somewhat higher than mid-distance between the hair line and the bridge of the nose, there is evidence of a gunshot wound (. . . injury no. 1). This wound is of an irregular shape: its right edge is arch-like and the left one is drawn in. One could not identify the size of it . . . The iris of the eye is clearly visible. Its size is 0.95 centimetres. Judging from its size, it is not difficult to determine the height of the forehead (the distance between the hair line and the bridge of the nose) and that the size of the wound is approx. 0.5 × 0.4 centimetres. Approximately 0.2 centimetres away from the right lower edge of the wound, there is a dark semicircle 0.15–0.20 centimetres wide. It could be a mark left by the muzzle of a gun, the so-called 'standsmark'.

In the region of the upper right part of the pubis there is an oval mark of 1.3 × 0.6 centimetres, which could be a bruise. There is a similar mark in the middle of the hair line.

The white of the right eye is very dark, suggesting a haemorrhage of the retina.

In the region of the inner corner of the right eye, the lower eyelid and the upper and outside part of the right jaw there is an S-shaped injury. It seems to be a bruise with the epicentre in the corner of the eye. Underneath it, in the middle of the right cheek, there are two scratches, one circular, approximately 0.5 × 0.5 centimetres, the other oval, 1.2 × 0.5 centimetres.

The nose looks a little squashed and deformed compared to the photo of Rasputin alive, especially the tip and the bridge. On the bridge of the nose, on the front and right parts of it, there are numerous scratches of irregular shape.

There is a Γ-shaped scratch on the right jaw [Γ is the fourth letter of the Cyrillic alphabet, equivalent to G in the Roman alphabet]. The right side of the forehead is bruised. Here, 2.5–3.0 centimetres above the outer corner of the right eye and 3–4 centimetres behind it, there are two scratches of irregular shape, approximately 1 × 1 centimetre and 0.8 × 0.8 centimetres.

... On the left side of the chest – equidistant between the left nipple and the rib curve – there is a wound of nearly oval shape, with injured skin around it (injury no. 2). The edges of the wound are jagged. The diameter of the wound is approximately two times bigger than the head of the match visible on the photo, which is about 0.3 centimetres, [and] approximately 1.2 times smaller than the diameter of the nipple, which is normally 0.6–0.7 centimetres. Thus the diameter of the wound is about 0.55–0.60 centimetres. Round the wound the colour of the skin is darker, especially towards the back of the body.

On the surface of the right side of the chest, at the level of the armpit, equidistant between imaginary lines from the nipple and the navel drawn perpendicular to the long axis of the body, there is a wound of an irregular oval shape with small protuberances of an irregular star shape (injury no. 3). Using the sizes of the head of the match and the nipple, one could determine the size of this wound: it is approximately 1.0 × 0.8 centimetres. Around this wound the skin is also darker, but less so than around the wound on the left.

On the back of the body in the lumbar region there is a wound of an irregular shape, the diameter of which is 1.5 times bigger than that of the head of the match (injury no. 4). One can assume that the diameter of this wound is about 0.45–0.50 centimetres. The edges of the wound cannot be seen clearly. The skin around it has normal colouration. There is also a wound with sharp and even edges approximately 2.7 centimetres long on the back of the body to the left of the spine. It is at 30 degrees to the vertical axis of the body (injury no. 5). It is a gaping wound. There is some discolouration of the skin next to the outer left edge of the wound.

Zharov then refers back to Kosorotov's findings:

According to Prof. Kosorotov, there were three gunshot wounds on the body. One of them, the chest one, damaged the stomach and the liver, the bullet going in and out of the body. The other one, in the back, caused damage to the right kidney.

. . . Having studied the photos we arrived at the conclusion that the wounds in the region of the chest to the left (injury no. 2) and to the right (injury no. 3), in the region of the forehead (injury no. 1) and in the back (injury no. 4) are of gunshot origin. After comparing the size, shape and character of the edges of these wounds [we can say] they are gunshot bullet wounds, while injury no. 3 is the wound where the bullet came out. So Prof. Kosorotov's opinion, which we support, is that the bullet in the back stayed in the body, while the bullet in the chest went through. As a result we conclude that the shot to the head was fired at close range (there appears to be a round 'standsmark' on the wound from the muzzle of the gun). Prof. Kosorotov does not mention in his report the bullet coming out of the head and there are no images of the back of the head on the photographs.

We do not have the data to establish the calibre of the weapon with which Rasputin was shot. We can only assume that the chest wound was caused by a 6.35mm gun or smaller. It could be, for example, a Browning No. 3 1906 model, a 'Baby' Browning or a Mauser 1910 model.

Wounds to the stomach and liver tend to cause shock and internal haemorrhaging. The wounded normally cannot move or be active. But sometimes a very fit person, especially under the moderate influence of alcohol, in extreme life-threatening circumstances, can actually walk or even run for a while, put up resistance and so on. So the actions of Rasputin, after he had been wounded in the stomach, as described by Yusupov and Purishkevich, could indeed have taken place.

As the forensic medicine shows, the bullet wounds in the head shot from close range caused severe destruction of the brain matter. Normally, immediately after a wound of such nature, there is a loss of consciousness and, as a result, an inability to perform any actions. The time it takes before the onset of death depends on which part of the brain is damaged and how badly. There is no mention of this on Prof. Kosorotov's report.

We agree with Prof. Kosorotov's opinion that the cause of death was not drowning and Rasputin was already dead when he was thrown into the water. Indeed Kosorotov confirms his opinion with some evidence (the lungs were not swollen and there was no water in the respiratory organs).

The question whether the bruises on the face were inflicted before or after Rasputin's death is impossible to answer, due to the lack of information. These injuries were caused by heavy, blunt objects. Rasputin was definitely hit more than once. Some injuries were inflicted when the body was thrown off the bridge. The presence of blood on the pylon of Petrovskii Bridge proves this. It is possible that the injuries on the face were caused by the blows of the rubber cane or weight, and the person who inflicted these injuries had his clothes covered in blood. The cut on the left side of the back (injury no. 5) was caused by a sharp object used only once (knife, razor etc). It is impossible to say whether this wound was inflicted before or after death.

They conclude:

It is possible that the lethal dose of potassium cyanide did not cause Rasputin's death. The poisoning did not occur, either as a result of cyanide changing its chemical status ... [text illegible] The nature of Rasputin's complaints about feeling unwell after he took the poisoned cakes and wine are characteristic of light poisoning. His autopsy showed three gunshot wounds where the bullets entered the body and one wound where the bullet came out; one cut and many bruises on the head caused by a heavy, blunt object. It is also impossible to conclude the sequence, and the distance, from which the shots were fired. We can only suppose that out of three gunshots, the one into the head was the last. This shot shows all the signs of being fired at close range. The shot into the chest was probably fired from quite a close distance as well. The mechanical injuries (the ones not caused by gunshots) in the region of the head were caused by a succession of blows inflicted by heavy, blunt objects. These injuries could not have been caused by the body hitting the pylon of the bridge from which it was thrown off. The cut on the back was caused by a sharp object, possibly a knife or a razor blade. It is not possible to say whether this injury happened before or after death. After Rasputin was wounded in his stomach and liver, it is possible that he could walk, run, put up resistance during the next 5–15 minutes. After he was wounded in the head, it is dubious that he was able to act with purpose and co-ordination. The injury most likely to have caused the death is the shot in the head, which caused the damage to the brain matter. There was no evidence of drowning in the materials studied.

As part of the *Timewatch* production I had the opportunity to interview Professor Zharov about his findings. A short excerpt from the interview is included in the transmitted programme. Three of the questions I asked Zharov and the answers he gave are, I believe, of particular importance.

'I wonder if you could give me your opinion about Professor Kosorotov's evidence that the three bullet wounds were caused by different-calibre weapons.'

'Yes, I think that is the case, if we accept the wound to the left side was caused by a Browning, the one to the back by a *Sauvage*, and then the one to the forehead was caused by a larger-calibre weapon than both of the other guns.'

'In your view does the contact wound to the forehead discredit Purishkevich's evidence?'

'Of course it does. Purishkevich said he fired at Rasputin from behind at a distance of twenty paces and hit Rasputin in the back of the head. The picture of Rasputin's forehead shows an entry wound; the standsmark around it means it was fired at close range.'

'In your view, as the forensic evidence tells us that three weapons of different calibre were used, does this mean that there was a third person involved in the shooting?'

'As a scientist I cannot say that a third person was involved in Rasputin's murder. What I can say is that as an individual I am certain someone else was involved, because neither Purishkevich nor Yusupov mention the close-quarter shot to the forehead. If they didn't do it, who did?'

So, to sum up Zharov's findings:

There is no forensic evidence that Rasputin was poisoned by the use of potassium cyanide (although the Zharov report identifies how the cyanide might have been neutralised). This is the problem of following what Yusupov and Purishkevich reported as fact. At the time of his demise Rasputin was in a state of drunkenness.

Rasputin did not die of drowning.

There is evidence that Rasputin was shot three times. All three weapons were fired from a range of no more than 20 centimetres. All three bullets were from different calibre weapons. It is impossible to know the sequence of the shots but the shot to the forehead would have been immediately disabling and was therefore in all likelihood the last. Both the shot to his left side (stomach/liver) and the one to the right side of his back (kidney) would individually have been fatal in 10–20 minutes.

The head and body had been beaten with a hard but supple weapon consistent with the cosh Yusupov refers to. The face was considerably disfigured. It is impossible to identify whether certain injuries were caused ante or post mortem, for instance hitting the bridge supports.

The exit wound for the shot to the left-hand side of the body is identified by Zharov and his colleagues as follows:

On the surface of the right side of the chest, at the level of the armpit, equidistant between imaginary lines from the nipple and the navel drawn perpendicular to the long axis of the body, there is a wound of an irregular oval shape with small protuberances of an irregular star shape.

The trajectory of the bullet is from the left side of the body at my calculated distance of approximately 13 centimetres below the nipple to the right chest at the level of the armpit, midway between straight horizontal lines drawn from the right nipple and the navel. The angle is approximately 30 degrees from the horizontal. The gun was therefore fired in an upwards direction.

Such a trajectory would damage firstly the stomach and then liver, as suggested by Kosorotov. In Figure 5, the black arrow marks the trajectory of the bullet once in the body and the point of the grey arrow marks the distance of 20 centimetres from the entry wound as evidenced by Kosorotov and also demonstrates the trajectory of the bullet before entering the body. If the shot was fired at a downward angle, as Andrew Cook suggests,[2] it would have missed the liver and probably the stomach. However, the trajectory of a bullet when it enters the body is often variable and dependent on a number of factors. All the same, I believe Kosorotov tells us the path the bullet followed – stomach then liver, which the upward trajectory shot would achieve.

Figure 5: Trajectory of bullet – left-hand side injury

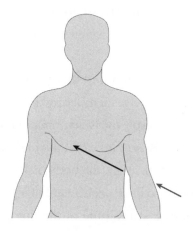

Support for Zharov's conclusion about the exit point of the bullet may be found in Plate 12, where there appears to be a large blood stain on the right-hand side of Rasputin's white shirt. This would be consistent with bleeding from the exit wound as described. As there are no other wounds in this region this is the most likely explanation.

The trajectory has considerable significance as it shows the shot was fired upwards from a position, by my calculation, almost exactly halfway between the armpit and the navel. How could such a shot be fired? In considering this piece of forensic evidence I have considered information from Joe Fuhrmann, who estimates Rasputin's height as between 5 feet 7 inches and 5 feet 8 inches (170–173 centimetres), and information from Greg King, who estimates Yusupov's height as no more than 5 feet 9 inches (175 centimetres).

I have attempted to reconstruct the shot using real people and have found that a standing shot at a 30 degree angle, using a 'victim' of 5 feet 8 inches and a 'conspirator' of 5 feet 9 inches requires the conspirator to move his arm and hand into the most bizarre position to deliver the shot from the left-hand side. The 'conspirator' would have to be right handed. I have always asserted that for this shot to be delivered Rasputin's left arm had to be raised to or above the height of the armpit, or his arms had to be tied behind his back, otherwise the bullet could not have entered without passing through the left arm.

It is also worth bearing in mind that if all three shots were fired more or less simultaneously, remembering there were three weapons used, the conspirators, respectively standing behind, in front of and to the left-hand side of Rasputin, would be in danger of being hit by a bullet passing straight through the body or head.

Kosorotov appears to have been aware of Yusupov's story, which was already circulating at the time of the autopsy, and this might have influenced his chronology of events and his approach to the post mortem.

Using Kosorotov's analysis and the details of Zharov's re-examination I analysed the size of the wound to the forehead. In April 2004 I wrote that it was consistent with wounds inflicted by a .455 Webley revolver. This was standard issue to the SIS and British officers at the time of Rasputin's murder. In early 2010 I asked Derrick Pounder, a professor of forensic medicine and one of the country's leading pathologists, to review his findings for the *Timewatch* programme and he concluded that he had no doubt the injury to the head, the *coup de grâce*, was caused by an unjacketed (lead) bullet of .455 calibre as used in the Webley revolver. He confirms that all the bullet wounds were close-range shots, the closest of which was the shot to the forehead.

*

Even in 1916 it would have been possible, had an analysis taken place, to establish whether the blood in the snow was human or canine or both. It would also have been possible for scientists to tell whether the blood in the snow had dripped, as from an inert body, or had splattered, as for instance if Rasputin had been running away across the yard.

Blood stains fall into three categories: passive (drops, pools etc.), transfer (for instance wiping a weapon) and projected (from bullets, stepping in blood). The last will often be seen in the form of an impact spatter, where the blood source is struck in some way and drops fly off in various directions. An example would be Rasputin being assaulted with a cosh. This category is further sub-divided into three categories: low velocity, where we find relatively large pools of blood, medium velocity, where blood is flicked off a blunt object for instance, and high velocity, for example where a firearm is used. Here the stains are often small.

So for example with the gunshot wound to the left side there would be blood staining at the entry point and at the exit point in the right centre of the chest. However, as we have no crime scene in the accepted sense, we cannot check for a spatter pattern.

Blood pattern analysis may on many occasions define the location of a victim or the assailant(s) by establishing the actions of either or both. Possible and impossible scenarios may be established to determine if the victim/witness/assailant is accurately describing what took place. An investigator would ask: What type of weapon or impact occurred to cause the blood stains present? How many times was the victim struck? Where was the victim at the time the injuries were inflicted? Where was the assailant during and following the assault? Is the blood stain evidence consistent with the pathologist's findings? Is the blood stain evidence on the suspect and his clothing consistent with the crime scene?

In this case we will never know the answer to these questions. However, we do know there would have been considerable blood; Zharov and his colleagues are quite clear that the extent of Rasputin's injuries from being beaten would have meant that his assailants were covered in blood.

CHAPTER NINE

DISMANTLING THE ACCEPTED VERSION OF EVENTS

Here I explore the discrepancies that I found in the accounts of Feliks Yusupov and Vladimir Purishkevich. I also take into account the witness evidence from the GARF records, the forensic evidence and my own assessment of the evidence.

If Feliks's wife Irina was to act as bait to entice Rasputin to the Yusupov Palace, why did Feliks tell his fellow conspirators, according to Purishkevich, on 22 November that Irina would not be in Petrograd on 16–17 December?

Vladimir Maklakov consistently denied providing Yusupov with the potassium cyanide; Maurice Paléologue states that it was provided by a doctor friend of Yusupov's from Obukhov Hospital. Purishkevich describes Yusupov handing Dr Lazovert potassium cyanide crystals, which Lazovert grated with a knife. They then went up to the study, where Yusupov handed Purishkevich and Grand Duke Dmitrii a phial of potassium cyanide solution. Yusupov contradicts this and claims that the potassium cyanide crystals were in a box that he took from the ebony cabinet in the dining room. Lazovert took the crystals out of the box and crushed them. In his initial memoirs Yusupov says the cyanide was grated into the chocolate petits fours; Purishkevich says the pink petits fours. Yusupov talks about cyanide being grated into the wine glasses, he later refers to phials. They disagree on the number of glasses that were poisoned: Purishkevich says two, Yusupov three. We are told there were four glasses in the room, but Yusupov uses five. The first, an unpoisoned glass, he gives to Rasputin; realising his error he contrives to drop it. He then gives Rasputin three glasses of wine each in a poisoned glass and has one himself.

Professor Kosorotov says there is no evidence of poisoning. The characteristic smell of almonds associated with potassium cyanide poisoning was not observed. Zharov confirms that Kosorotov does not note the smell of almonds.

There are considerable differences in the accounts of when Petrovskii Bridge over the Malaya Nevka was identified as being suitable because of an 'ice hole' for the disposal of Rasputin's body.

Yusupov describes Dmitrii and his guests arriving at the Moika palace together. Purishkevich elaborately describes the side gates to the yard being locked, his gaining access through the main entrance, and Yusupov scurrying away to make sure the side gates were duly opened. Yusupov himself makes no mention of this. Ivan Nefedov tells us that Dmitrii Pavlovich arrived through the front door between 11.00 p.m. and midnight on 16 December, or so he was told by Buzhinskii, Yusupov's butler. If Dmitrii had arrived by car, why did he not leave his car in the yard of 92 Moika Embankment, or in the main courtyard of the palace, as it was to be used later in the night to take Rasputin's body to the Malaya Nevka?

Purishkevich describes his own car, and the painting over of his family motto to prevent identification by police. The car was covered, as identified by Purishkevich and the witness Fyodor Antonovich Korshunov, who describes it as 'a large car . . . khaki in colour [with] a canvas top and safety glass windows'. Yusupov describes the car as open, giving this as the reason that Dmitrii's closed car was used to take the body to the Malaya Nevka. Purishkevich says Dmitrii's car was used because the police would know it and not stop it. He contradicts this later on by saying that Dmitrii was driving slowly to avoid attracting the attention of the police.

Korshunov, the yard keeper for 64 Gorokhovaya Street, Rasputin's address, does not describe Yusupov as being either of the two men who turned up to collect Rasputin. He describes the person who went in to get Rasputin as 'above average height, medium build, about thirty years of age, small black moustache, no beard, I think no glasses, was wearing a long expensive fur coat, with fur outside, and a black hat, which I did not see well. He was wearing high boots.' Yusupov was twenty-nine years of age in 1916, but photographs taken of him then show he had no moustache, nor does the rest of Korshunov's description match with Yusupov.

Akim Lazukov, the yard keeper at 92 Moika Embankment, tells Colonel Popel' of the Detached Gendarme Corps that there was no car in the yard at the time he heard the shots.

At the Yusupov Palace, Yusupov and Purishkevich disagree in the positioning of the crucifix in the basement dining room, and on the number of times Yusupov went up from the basement room to his study: Purishkevich describes in detail three occasions, whereas Yusupov says he went up only once. He claims that he sang and played his guitar for Rasputin but that this was unheard by his attentive fellow conspirators assembled at the top of the stairs.

In Yusupov's final visit to the study (according to Purishkevich), or in his own account his only visit, joint action by the conspirators against Rasputin is proposed. Purishkevich suggests that Dmitrii pulled the conspirators back from this course of action when they had gone five steps down the staircase. Yusupov says he convinced his friends with great difficulty that he should carry out the murder alone.

Much of what Purishkevich said was heard, such as corks being taken out of bottles, is beyond belief. Yusupov and Rasputin were in the basement drawing room, two flights of stairs and three doors from where Purishkevich and the other conspirators were allegedly waiting in Yusupov's study. Although Purishkevich says he and the others came down the stairs to listen how far did they come? Was it to the landing by the yard door, halfway down the stairs, or beyond that point? The gramophone was playing; for how long? The same tune repeated? Could they hear anything over the noise of the record? Yusupov even tells us that his co-conspirators were becoming restless and he could hear them downstairs.

Moving on to the issue of whose gun, Yusupov says Dmitrii handed him his (Dmitrii's) Browning; Purishkevich says Yusupov took his own 'pocket' Browning from his desk drawer. We have already discussed the practicalities of walking backwards and concealing the weapon behind one's back – how did Yusupov pour the wine?

If as Yusupov asserts the first shot was to Rasputin's left side, Yusupov must have been standing to Rasputin's left. If the room was laid out as per the current exhibit in the Yusupov Palace then Rasputin would have needed to fall to the left, towards Yusupov and past him to land on the 'white bearskin rug' on which both Yusupov and Purishkevich say the body landed. This does not fit with Yusupov's assertion that Rasputin gave a cry and 'crumpled' up on the rug. Lazovert appears to indicate that all the conspirators were in the room when the shot was fired.

Purishkevich says:

I stood over Rasputin watching him intently. He was not yet dead. He was breathing in agony. He had covered both his eyes and half of his long spongy nose with his right hand. His left arm was stretched along his body, and every now and then, his chest rose high and his body twitched convulsively. We left the dining room, turning out the light and leaving the door slightly ajar.

Contrast this with Yusupov:

Rasputin lay on his back. His features twitched in nervous spasms; his hands were clenched, his eyes closed. A blood stain was spreading on his silk blouse. A few moments later all movement ceased. We bent over his body to examine it . . . There was no possibility of doubt: Rasputin was dead . . . We turned off the light and went up to my room, after locking the basement door.

Well, at least they agree that the light was turned off! One has Rasputin alive and the door left ajar, the other has Rasputin dead and the door locked!

As for Rasputin's resurrection, after Rasputin allegedly recovered from his first gunshot wound, Purishkevich describes a hysterical Yusupov running up from the basement dining room and through to his parents' apartments in the palace. Yusupov himself says he went up to the study, picked up his cosh and led Purishkevich, who was armed with his Savage pistol, downstairs. Yusupov, who must have forced his way past the following Purishkevich on the basement stairs, then rushes through the main entrance of the palace and runs along the Moika side of the yard fence to head Rasputin off. Purishkevich makes no mention of this activity on the stairs; in his version Yusupov is not there.

Purishkevich pursues Rasputin into the yard, fires two shots, misses, bites his hand to make himself concentrate and then fires twice again, twenty paces distant from the fleeing Rasputin, hitting him firstly in the back and then in the head. Lazovert has Rasputin crawling and, incidentally, so does Paléologue. The forensic evidence establishes this as a lie.

The considered opinion of Kosorotov does not coincide with Yusupov's and Purishkevich's accounts. He says the shot to Rasputin's side was fired from a range of no more than 20 centimetres (8 inches). The wound to the right side of the back he says was fired shortly afterwards, and the forensic evidence establishes that this bullet was fired from an equally close range. The shot to the head was fired almost from 'contact' range or, if not, extremely close range and bears evidence of the characteristic 'standsmark'. The forensic evidence is that the wounds were caused by three weapons of different calibres – not, as suggested by Yusupov and Purishkevich, two, a Browning and a Savage.

Purishkevich says he stayed by the body for some minutes and kicked the prostrate Rasputin in the temple. He did not see Yusupov! Yusupov says he saw Purishkevich and shouted to him, but Purishkevich did not respond. Given the relatively small size of the yard at 92 Moika Embankment it is highly unlikely that Purishkevich would not have heard or seen Yusupov.

Had Yusupov's account of running alongside the yard been true he would have been close to Purishkevich when he allegedly fired the two shots that knocked Rasputin to the floor. I agree with Professor Zharov that the distance from the wall of the palace to the main gates of the yard at 92 Moika Embankment is no more than 20 metres. There was no wall, just iron fencing.

Yusupov tells us that he ran alongside the fence of 92 Moika Embankment towards the middle gates of the yard 'because only the middle gates were unlocked'. How does this relate with Purishkevich's statement about using the side gates? If Lazovert drove Yusupov and Rasputin through the side gates then who locked them afterwards? From which gate did the other conspirators leave on their way to Purishkevich's train at the Warsaw railway station and to collect Dmitrii's car? Who locked the side gates after they left?

However, Yusupov was in the yard when the policeman Stepan Vlasyuk arrived; the body was allegedly still in the yard and shielded from Vlasyuk's view by Yusupov and his major-domo. This represents a phenomenal turn of speed by Vlasyuk, given that Purishkevich says that after standing by the body for just a few minutes he went inside and sent Nefedov and Buzhinskii out to drag the body indoors. Vlasyuk, according to his statement was at his post at the junction of Prachechnyi Lane and Maksimilianovskii Lane when he heard the 'shots'. He then made his way via Prachechnyi Lane across Pochtamtskii Bridge and spoke to Yefimov at his post near 61 Bol'shaya Morskaya Street. Vlasyuk covered some considerable distance and yet according to Yusupov the body was still in the yard. You will recall he suggests that as Vlasyuk approached, he was standing in front of the body and the two servants were running out into the yard.

Vlasyuk tells a different story. He says that Yusupov and Buzhinskii were walking across the yard towards him together. He would have been in an ideal position to see the body if it was there. He goes on to say that after the conversation in the yard Yusupov and Buzhinskii left while he remained and looked around; he did not see the corpse. A corpse against the white snow is going to be highly visible with, even on a dark and bleak December night, the street lighting casting sufficient light for Vlasyuk to see any body lying on the ground.

We now move on to Vlasyuk's return to the Moika palace. Purishkevich states that this was after Yusupov physically assaulted Rasputin's corpse; Yusupov suggests it was before he went down to Rasputin's lifeless body. Purishkevich recalls Yusupov being dragged off the body by the two servants; Yusupov states that he fell asleep by the body and was taken to bed by Purishkevich and Nefedov.

Purishkevich mentions how Yusupov was blood stained from the assault and seated in the study on a sofa. He was still in this position when Vlasyuk returned. Vlasyuk contradicts this, stating that as he entered Yusupov's study Purishkevich and Yusupov walked towards him. He does not mention Yusupov's clothes being blood stained. Purishkevich says that he asked Buzhinskii to recall Vlasyuk. Vlasyuk says that Buzhinskii told him that it was Yusupov who asked him to return. Yusupov says that Buzhinskii told him that Vlasyuk had been told to return because his initial report was considered insufficient. There could be correlation with Paléologue's comments about a member of the Okhrana being present, although this is highly improbable.

The scene-of-crime photograph (Plate 7) clearly shows a line of blood spots in the snow. What it also shows is snow piled up against the side gate, which was allegedly open on the night. A telegram to the headquarters of the supreme commander of the Russian armed forces states: 'Traces of blood had been found on the snow in the small garden in the course of close examination.'[1] There is clearly a covering of snow on the yard, to which Purishkevich refers. Had the gate been open and the snow not piled up against it on the night of the murder the blood would have been swept up to a greater degree with the snow. I believe this shows conclusively the side gates were never opened on the night of the murder.

Turning to the weights and chains, in his diary entry (if it was a diary) for 29 November, Purishkevich states that he and his wife purchased the two pood weights and chains to send Rasputin's body to the bottom of the river. As an aside the thought of Mr and Mrs Purishkevich carrying these heavy weights through the streets of Petrograd is almost farcical. We hear no more of these weights and chains until Purishkevich tells us that Rasputin's body was dragged into Dmitrii's car on the night of the murder. He suggests that he brought them to the Yusupov Palace that night but he makes no mention about this as he describes his and Lazovert's arrival at the palace.

The farce of the cars – Purishkevich tells us that Dmitrii, Sergei Sukhotin and Lazovert, with Lazovert dressed as the chauffeur and Sukhotin wearing Rasputin's outer clothes to fool police spies, drive to Purishkevich's train. Here we are told Mrs Purishkevich and Mrs Lazovert were to burn the clothing. Because it is difficult Mrs Purishkevich declines. The three load Purishkevich's car onto a railway truck and then either take a cab or walk to the Belosel'skii-Belozerskii Palace on Nevskii Avenue to collect Dmitrii's car, carrying all Rasputin's clothes with them. Lazovert does not mention this cross-Petrograd trip.

The application of real timings to the alleged sequence of events and journeys undertaken expose this part of Purishkevich's and Yusupov's stories to be a total fabrication. Even being generous with the timings, the earliest Purishkevich and Lazovert could have finally returned to the Warsaw station was 7.00 a.m. and not sometime after 5.00, as Purishkevich suggests.

The bound body of Rasputin was dragged into the back of Dmitrii's car. The grand duke drove and Sukhotin sat next to him. Purishkevich sat on the left in the back, with Lazovert on the right. The body is on the floor with Nefedov sitting on top of it. Rather cramped? It was even more cramped than this: there were the two pood weights to be accommodated, plus Rasputin's beaver coat and so on.

The body would have bled profusely yet there is only one line of blood in the yard. According to Purishkevich, Rasputin ran across the yard while bleeding; he was shot twice and collapsed in the snow. He was dragged back across the yard to the basement, and then out to the car. There are no irregular patterns of blood dripping that would have been associated with such movements of the body.

The car must have been so spacious that when they arrived at Petrovskii Bridge, they failed to notice and forgot to attach the weights and chains to Rasputin's body. They also forgot the fur coat and galoshes. One of the galoshes they wouldn't discover until their return to Dmitrii's residence. Purishkevich says that after the body was thrown into the river, they realised they hadn't thrown the coat in, so they weighted it with the chains and threw it in after the body. This could not have been right as the coat was wrapped around the body when it was recovered. Rasputin had been dead for some time when he entered the water. He did not attempt to release his bonds.

Both Yusupov and Purishkevich claim that they had to hurry to remove the body as 'dawn was approaching'; in fact it was still some hours away.

A farce of a tale and a farcical investigation

In addition to Yusupov, Dmitrii, Purishkevich, Lazovert and Sukhotin, who else knew of the plot to kill? In no particular order these are: Yusupov's wife Irina and his mother; Mrs Purishkevich; Mrs Lazovert; Maklakov; Mikhail Rodzyanko, the president of the Duma, and his wife; Oswald Rayner of the British Special Intelligence Service and thus his fellow agents John Scale and Stephen Alley (Purishkevich even told Sir Samuel Hoare of the plan); Fyodor,

Yusupov's brother-in-law; Dmitrii's valet; V. V. Shulgin, deputy in the Second, Third and Fourth Dumas.

In fact, the list is likely to be substantially longer, as Yusupov tells us:

> I imagined that it would be easy to find a few determined men ready to help me to find a way of eliminating Rasputin. The conversation I had on the subject with different influential people left me with few illusions. The very men who were the most violent whenever the *starets*'s name was mentioned became reticent at once when I told them the time had come to act.

Strange, is it not, that the Tsar's secret police, the Okhrana, were unaware of the plot with so many people being aware of it?

The pledge of secrecy that the conspirators committed to lasted for a day at the most; Paléologue reported in detail an account of the murder that almost coincides with the broad story of the conspirators. George Buchanan, the British ambassador, knew that Rasputin was missing on 17 December. Purishkevich, if he is to be believed, kept a diary and went to print in 1918. Yusupov followed suit in 1927, the book being translated by his intimate friend Rayner.

Dmitrii never spoke to Yusupov after the publication of his 1927 book. Purishkevich had died in 1920, but a reprint of his diary appeared in 1923, and Lazovert told his brief tale of the murder in the same year. Dmitrii and Sukhotin, as far as we know, never told their side of the tale.

I have assessed the evidence of the witnesses, including the known conspirators, identifying their credibility as witnesses in a criminal trial in Table 2.

Table 2: Assessment of witnesses' evidence

Witness	Role	Credibility
Feliks Yusupov	Conspirator	Perjured
Vladimir Purishkevich	Conspirator	Perjured
Stanislaus de Lazovert	Conspirator	Doubtful
Sergei Sukhotin	Conspirator	No evidence
Dmitrii Pavlovich	Conspirator	No evidence
Maurice Paléologue	French ambassador	Hearsay
Nikolai Mikhailovich	Grand duke	Hearsay
Albert Stopford		Hearsay

Evidence as to 'shots' at Moika

Stepan Vlasyuk	Police officer	Good witness
Flor Yefimov	Police officer	Good witness
Akim Lazukov	Yard keeper	Suborned
Ul'yan Bobkov	Watchman	Suborned
Ivan Nefedov	Batman	Suborned

Collection of Rasputin from 64 Gorokhovaya Street

Fyodor Korshunov	Yard keeper	Fair witness
Yekaterina Poterkina	Maid	Fair witness

Recovery of clothing etc. at Petrovskii Bridge

Fyodor Kuz'min	Bridge guard	Good witness
Vasilii Kordukov	Policeman	Good witness
Asonov	Police inspector	Good witness
Mikhailov	Police inspector	Good witness

A post mortem cut short and an aborted murder investigation

We know that the post mortem was conducted in poor conditions and dim light. By order of the Empress there was no analysis of the samples taken from Rasputin, not that I believe they would have helped substantially other than to dispel the suggestion that he was poisoned. My stance is that the evidence of Professor Kosorotov and our current knowledge of forensic medicine allows us to say conclusively he was not poisoned. Kosorotov looked for poison because the story was out that the conspirators had first tried to poison Rasputin.

I have heard some references to the extensive investigations of various police officials in 1916–17. I have to say I am totally unimpressed by them all. As incompetent as the murder was, the investigations have all the hallmarks of a farce. It may well be that the Tsar's prerogative was used to halt the investigation but one has the sense that Colonel Popel' of the Detached Gendarme Corps and Major General Popov did not put too much effort into challenging Yusupov and others over the events of 16–17 December 1916.

Vlasyuk's concerns about the shots he heard fired led to the matter being reported to higher authorities. By 5.00 a.m. (Vlasyuk's timing), Inspector Kalyadich had arrived on the scene at 92–94 Moika Embankment. He had spoken to Lazukov and was on his way to speak to Yusupov. Vlasyuk had asked Buzhinskii to ensure Yusupov waited for Kalyadich. Instead Yusupov drove off in his car. Yusupov had lied to Vlasyuk in the yard of No. 92 when he and Buzhinskii hadn't heard shots. We know that Lazukov lied to Vlasyuk in his oral statement of 17 December. When interviewed the next day he told Popel' that he heard two 'not very loud' shots.

Ivan Nefedov was interviewed on 17 December, whereas the majority of witnesses were interviewed on 18 December. What might Popel' have reasonably known by the time he interviewed Nefedov? He had the oral evidence on Vlasyuk and Yefimov (statements were taken on 18 December), but it is clear from Vlasyuk's statement that he had been interviewed on 17 December and shown a photograph of Purishkevich. Popel' knew that Yusupov had allegedly had guests for the evening/night. We know that Rasputin left his apartment at or about midnight on 16 December. It is clear that Popel' knew by 17 December, either from Yekaterina Poterkina, the yard keeper at 64 Gorokhovaya Street, or from Rasputin's daughter, that Rasputin had been waiting to be picked up by Yusupov, or that Yusupov had actually attended the flat. Depending on the time of day that Nefedov's statement was taken he may or may not have been aware that blood had been found on Petrovskii Bridge and that Rasputin's overshoe had been found on the ice (at 2.00 p.m. by Kuz'min's timing).

However, where did Popel' get the intelligence that led him to ask Nefedov whether he had heard shots in the dining room? There being no specific evidence to suggest that shots had been fired in the basement, did he make a lucky guess or did he have intelligence? Was 94 Moika Embankment, as Paléologue suggests, being kept under surveillance by an Okhrana agent? After interviewing Nefedov, who had confirmed the basement party, Popel' seems to have done nothing about visiting what may have been a possible crime scene in the basement dining room, or did he?

In her book *Memories of the Russian Court*, Anna Vyrubova asserted:

> The police, at their commands, went to the deserted Yusupov palace,
> first searching for and finding the body of the dog which Feliks said

they had shot. But the bullet hole in the dog's head had let out little blood, and when the men entered the palace they found it a veritable shambles of blood and disorder. Evidence of a terrific struggle were found in the downstairs study of Prince Feliks, on the stairs leading to an upper room, and in the room itself. Then, indeed, the whole power of the police was invoked, and somebody was found to testify that in the dead of night a motor car without any lights was seen leaving the Yusupov Palace and disappearing in the direction of the Neva. Winter nights in Russia are very dark, as everyone knows, and the car was soon swallowed up in the shadows.[2]

Of course this does not coincide with Nefedov's account, which said he had tidied up the basement room. Nor does it coincide with Yusupov's account, where he has himself and Nefedov tidying the basement, cleaning up the blood on the stairs and so on. You will recall he even says that the following day he and Nefedov found more marks and cleaned them up.

Yusupov goes on to state (17 December) that the Chief Commissioner of Police, General Balk,

warned me that the Empress had given orders to search our house on the Moika. The fact that the shots fired there coincided with Rasputin's disappearance seemed, to say the least of it, suspicious. I answered, 'Our house is occupied by my wife. She is the Emperor's niece, and residences of the imperial family may not be searched without an order from the Emperor himself.' The commissioner was obliged to agree, and cancelled the search warrant on the spot.

Would there have not been intelligence on the whereabouts of Irina? In any case she was not seen by Vlasyuk, and Yusupov left on his own at around 4.00–5.00 a.m. Certainly in his statement of 18 December he makes no pretence that Irina was at the palace on the night of the murder. In fact he goes so far as to say: 'However, I did not want to introduce Rasputin to my household. I had the rooms at my Moika house, No. 94, urgently refurbished and Grand Duke Dmitrii Pavlovich suggested having a house-warming party.'

When Major General Popov interviewed Yusupov he would have known that: Yusupov had lied to Vlasyuk in the yard at their first meeting; Grand Duke Dmitrii and Purishkevich were amongst the guests in the basement dining room; Yusupov had allegedly been at Rasputin's flat; Rasputin's boot etc. had been found and identified by relatives. He had the evidence of Purishkevich's comments to Vlasyuk in the study and he knew of Yusupov's story about the dog. However, it appears that Yusupov was not challenged about his evidence and the case was left in abeyance until the Tsar arrived.

Rasputin's deep-frozen body was subsequently recovered from the Malaya Nevka. The post mortem, once the body had defrosted, was carried out in less than ideal circumstances, but it did at least reveal some facts, facts that might have been confirmed if the body had not been exhumed by the Bolsheviks from its grave in Anna Vyrubova's chapel at Tsarskoe Selo. The body was allegedly incinerated at the roadside, but of this there is no proof, other than testimony.

CHAPTER TEN

WHO DID AND WHO DIDN'T KILL RASPUTIN?

In discovering who did kill Rasputin we first of all need to identify who didn't kill him. The traditional and accepted version is contained in the memoirs of Yusupov (in its various forms) and Purishkevich. Lazovert's short version of events is rarely referred to. For too long these versions have been accepted as fact and their contents not challenged to any great extent. It is a great story, befitting of a great storyteller or dramatist, so why challenge it?

It is only recently that there have been challenges to what happened at the Moika palace on the night of 16–17 December. Oleg Shishkin comes close to identifying what happened and for the first time raises the issue of the shot to the forehead.[1] He identifies the murderer as Samuel Hoare, at the time head of station of the British SIS in Petrograd. He relies on the fact that Hoare was an Oxford graduate (New College) and therefore fitted the description of the individual believed by the Tsar to have been involved in the killing. The Tsar put this directly to George Buchanan, the British ambassador to the Romanov Court, describing an individual as 'Yusupov's Oxford University friend'; Buchanan on Hoare's briefing denied British involvement. Hoare's time at Oxford predated

Yusupov's, which coincided with Oswald Rayner's, although they were at different colleges.

Edvard Radzinskii, by trade a playwright, makes a drama over the involvement of Grand Duke Dmitrii, who he suggests is the murderer. His books are engrossing but attract more than their fare share of attention, while other, more accurate books, by other authors, are overlooked and, if written in Russian, are rarely translated. Unfortunately he has based his assertions on his partial use of evidence contained in the GARF files and has constructed a story that has not one shred of evidence to support it. He does not, despite his extensive research, address the fatal bullet wound to the forehead. He asserts that 'the vestiges of truth, in my view, are to be found in Feliks's first testimony given immediately after the murder'. This is a ridiculous suggestion. Yusupov shows himself to be an inveterate liar.

Not having access to the Museum of Political History or the Russian archives, many have willingly accepted Radzinskii's version of Rasputin's murder as substantiated fact; it is not. It is both subjective and speculative. The lie has always been exposed from the time of Kosorotov's post mortem and the fact that Rasputin had been shot through the head at point blank range was leaked to the extent that Albert Stopford writes about it in his diaries.

Radzinskii in my view takes the parts of the evidence, some of it hearsay, that suit his story but ignores much of what is in the GARF statements. He tries to make the case that Dmitrii was an expert marksman, which he was, but discredits Purishkevich's ability to shoot. However, Purishkevich tells us: 'I was a better than average shot; I regularly practised shooting small targets on the firing range at the Semyonovskii parade ground, but today I was not able to lay out a man at twenty paces.' The forensic evidence shows clearly that

Rasputin was shot at close range. So Radzinskii perpetuates the myth of firing across the yard but replaces Purishkevich with Dmitrii.

Radzinskii becomes confusing about the car(s); at one stage he says Dmitrii could not have left the palace and returned because no car was seen at the palace but then he falsely suggests, in respect of the police constables' evidence: 'The only thing they noticed was an automobile leaving the house after the shots, the one in which Rasputin's corpse was carried away.' This is incorrect; Flor Yefimov says a car drove past the palace along Moika Embankment without stopping, travelling from the Blue Bridge towards the Neva, and Vlasyuk tells us that Yusupov left the palace some time later in the prince's car. Radzinskii also refers to the telegram of General Globachyov, the head of the Okhrana, on 18 December: 'Several shots rang out, a human cry was heard, and later a car drove away.'

We need to carefully examine what Globachyov says in his telegram. You will see that it is substantially inaccurate when compared to the statements of the witnesses of which it is meant to be a composite. It is a shorthand version of what happened. You need to compare it with the detailed statements of witnesses such as Yefimov and Vlasyuk. The issue about the man firing the shot in the courtyard being in military field dress appears in none of the witness statements. Neither does the fact that later a car drove away appear in the statements – two cars are described, one that drives straight past the palace without stopping and the other, Yusupov's, leaving the front door in Vlasyuk's presence. For the purpose of completeness the telegram is reproduced in full below:

> On the night from the sixteenth to the seventeenth the point duty policeman heard several revolver shots near 94 Moika, owned by Prince Yusupov. Soon after that the policeman was invited to the study of the

young Prince Yusupov, where the prince and a stranger who called himself Purishkevich were present. The latter said: 'I am Purishkevich. Rasputin has perished. If you love the Tsar and fatherland you will keep silent.' The policeman reported this to his superiors. The investigation conducted this morning established that one of Yusupov's guests had fired a shot in the small garden adjacent to No. 94 at around 3 a.m. The garden has a direct entrance to the prince's study. A human scream was heard and following that a sound of a car being driven away. The person who had fired the shot was wearing a military field uniform. Traces of blood have been found on the snow in the small garden in the course of close examination. When questioned by the governor of the city, the young prince stated that he had had a party that night, but that Rasputin was not there, and that Grand Duke Dmitrii Pavlovich had shot a watchdog. The dog's body was found buried in the snow. The investigation conducted at Rasputin's residence at 64 Gorokhovaya Street established that at 10 p.m. on 16 December Rasputin said that he was not going to go out any more that night and was going to sleep. He let off his security and the car in his normal fashion. Questioning the servants and the yard keeper allowed police to establish that at 12:30 a.m. a large canvas-top car with driver and a stranger in it arrived at the house. The stranger entered Rasputin's apartment through the back door. It seemed that Rasputin was expecting him because he greeted him as somebody he knew and soon went outside with him through the same entrance. Rasputin got into the car, which drove off along Gorokhovaya Street towards Morskaya Street. Rasputin has not returned home and has not been found despite the deployed measures. There are many reasons to assume that he had been assassinated in Yusupov's garden and his body had been taken out of the city and hidden. The judicial inquest has not been opened due to the absence of the object of the offence; still the investigation in accordance with

Article 23 of the Martial Law has been assigned by the Minister of Internal Affairs to Commission General Popov. On receipt of new information will send a supplementary wire.

We then move on to the vexed issue of the ladies who were allegedly at the palace that night, for which there is not one shred of primary evidence. Basically Radzinskii suggests that Dmitrii is in the yard of No. 92 with the two ladies, Purishkevich chases Rasputin into the yard and fires two shots that miss, and Dmitrii then shoots Rasputin. We do not know where he was standing and would Purishkevich really fire off two shots into a yard in which two ladies were standing? I think not.

He proposes that the others took the blame so 'the hands of the royal youth' had not been 'stained with . . . blood'. This is nonsense. Dmitrii had touched the dead body, he had moved it off the 'white bearskin rug', so we are told. In legal terms he was as guilty as his fellow conspirators, as guilty as if he had fired the fatal shots. In one account he supplied the gun, touched the body and used his car to dispose of the body.

Radzinskii uses the well-known letter below that was written to Irina, who was in the Crimea at the time where she and their child were unwell. He also says that the letter was written to Irina on the day Yusupov met Purishkevich for the first time. From Purishkevich's diary we know this to be 21 November. The letter reads:

I'm terribly busy working on a plan to eliminate Rasputin. That is simply essential now, since otherwise everything will be finished. For that, I often see M. [Mariya] Gol.[ovina] and him [Rasputin]. They've grown quite fond of me and are forthcoming about everything with me. You too must take part in it. Dm.[itrii] Pavl.[ovich] knows all

187

about it and is helping. It will take place in the middle of December, when Dm. comes back . . . How much I want to see you before that. But it will be better if you do not come earlier, since the rooms won't be ready until 15 December, and not even all of them. And you won't have anywhere to stay. Not a word to anyone about what I've written.

And the equally well-published reply:

Many thanks for your mad letter. I could not understand half of it, but I can see that you are preparing for some wild action. Please, be careful, and don't mix yourself up in any bad business. My chief objection is that you have decided upon everything without consulting me. I don't see what use I can be now once everything has been fixed. That is disgusting of you. Who is this M. Gol.? This is what you write about him: 'For this reason I frequently see M. Gol. and him.' I have just understood what these words mean, and who the people are, this very minute while I was writing. In a word, be careful! I can see by your letter that you are wildly enthusiastic, and ready to climb up walls.

I intend going to Kiev with Mamma. She will probably go on 6 or 7 December; on the 12th or 13th I shall be in Petrograd. Don't you dare to do anything without me, or I shall not come at all!

On 27 November Feliks wrote back to Irina:

Your presence in the middle of December is essential. The plan I'm writing to you about has been worked out in detail and is three quarters done, and only the finale is left, and for that your arrival is awaited. It is the only way of saving a situation that is almost hopeless. You will serve as the lure. Of course not a word to anyone.

Malanya also taking part.

Purishkevich tells us that on 21 November he had gone to Yusupov's palace and Yusupov told the conspirators:

> The countess is not in Petrograd now. She is in the Crimea and hasn't the slightest intention of returning to Petrograd. However, on my last visit with Rasputin I told him that she would be returning to the capital soon for a few days and that if he, Rasputin, wanted, I would arrange for him to meet her at my home one evening when she would be visiting my parents.

But, as we know, Irina never did come to Petrograd to participate as the lure for the murder.

Radzinskii suggests that two women were at the palace; Yusupov declared in his statement to Popov that there were women at the palace that night but he refused to name them. The first woman Radzinskii suggests was present at the palace is Vera Karalli, a ballerina who had gone out with Dmitrii Pavlovich. It is not difficult to find a link between the two and she is mentioned in Dmitrii's April 1917 letter to Yusupov quoted in Chapter 4. Radzinskii outlines how she appeared in many police reports as being suspected of being at the palace. But the fact is there is not one shred of evidence to support his contention. In fact the police investigation showed that she was at her hotel that night and had not checked out. In a fantastic twist it is suggested that another woman took her place at the hotel and she sneaked out to be present at the murder – high drama, worthy of one of his novels. There is no evidence at all to support this outrageous and fanciful claim.

Radzinskii names the other woman suspect as Marianna Derfelden, née Pistohlkors – claiming she is in fact the 'Malanya' referred to in Yusupov's letter of 27 November. Marianna was

Grand Duke Pavel's step-daughter. In fact there is no evidence against her, but to support his contention Radzinskii explains that Aron Simanovich, Rasputin's secretary, who allegedly visited the Moika police station on 17 December, claimed she was involved. To be honest this is scraping the barrel for supportive evidence – Simanovich, in my view and the view of many others, is utterly discreditable and nothing he says can be relied on as being the truth.

Andrew Cook suggests that Rasputin was taken to the basement dining room, was beaten up, escaped and ran out to the yard.[2] Someone who was standing in Yusupov's study, looking out into the yard of 92 Moika Embankment, saw Rasputin escaping and fired through the window out into the dark yard. Cook bases this argument on the fact that one of the scene-of-crime photographs shows what appears to be a broken window that has been boarded up in the study. What he manages to skip over is that there is no suggestion that glass was found in the snow when detectives visited the scene; rather surprising, one might think? They found blood but no glass. Neither Vlasyuk nor Yefimov mentions hearing glass breaking, or the other shots Stopford refers to. Shooting from light (the study) into darkness (the yard) is very, very difficult – even if you can see your target.

This theory suggests that Rasputin, being scared, dropped down on the snow and that some time later one or more of the conspirators dragged him back to the palace. Apparently Rasputin running from the palace dripping blood would account for the blood in the snow. So I suppose that the conspirators dragged him back following exactly the same route so as not to create another trail of blood? Blood shows well when a person is dragged if they are bleeding profusely; it leaves a distinctive pattern. The theory then suggests that Rasputin was carried back out into the yard with his hands bound and propped, and sat down against the snow pile at the spot where the large area of blood is found on the photographs. You must remember that this all allegedly went on after the police, according to Stopford and others, had already visited the palace because of the shots fired from the study window. Really? Wouldn't the police be on the alert? Yefimov and Vlasyuk seem to me to be quite alert. There is no reason not to fully accept the evidence of the two police officers.

It is suggested Rasputin was then shot by two people, presumably the left-hand side body shot first. Firstly the snow pile was at most 24 inches (60 centimetres) high (calculated against the height of the fence, which is just over 6 feet or 180 centimetres tall) and less in fact where the large area of blood staining was found. So there he is sitting against the snow and shot 1 is fired. If Professor Zharov is right, this was an upward shot and therefore the person who fired must have been lying down. If, as Cook suggests, the shot was downward then Rasputin must have had his hands tied behind his back – otherwise it would have been impossible to get the shot in, unless you lifted the arm. The body topples forward and shot 2 is fired by another gunman, but from where? Was he standing on the snow pile, to the side? It doesn't add up. It is further suggested that Rasputin was then wrapped up in the cloth, but we don't know where; in the yard in front of the police, who have now heard more shots? I think not. Or was he dragged back to the palace and wrapped up, with yet more trails of blood? To finish it off he was carried back out into the yard groaning, and then the *coup de grâce* was delivered to the head. The police, who by Stopford's accounts are so interested, do nothing. It is strange that Vlasyuk and Yefimov do not mention any of this, nor is it mentioned in the official report previously referred to.

In the *Timewatch* programme I suggested that the two shots to the body were fired in the basement and that after being 'mummified'

Rasputin was taken into the yard and here the *coup de grâce* was delivered. I now realise that that conclusion was wrong. My continued and more detailed research leads me to conclude that all three shots were fired in the basement room, where the whole lurid torture and murder of Rasputin took place.

Those who want to believe the fantasy of a heroic Dmitrii taking the life of Rasputin would do well to reflect on the above. It was not Dmitrii. He was there; of that there is no doubt. Radzinskii suggests that Dmitrii could not be identified as being involved in the murder or handling the body. Despite Radzinskii's manoeuvring around this issue, Dmitrii did, if we are to believe the accounts of Yusupov and Purishkevich, lay hands on the dying peasant: he moved the body from the white bearskin rug after Yusupov shot him so no blood would seep onto the rug. Yusupov and Purishkevich are explicit about this – but somehow Radzinskii interposes Yusupov for Dmitrii in his account. The story about the women is also nonsense, as is Radzinskii's hypothesis around the chain of events and Dmitrii's involvement.

Imperial law protected Dmitrii from prosecution without the Tsar's specific consent and Nicholas would never have given such consent. Dmitrii knew he was safe but the Tsar's banishment of him was his sanction for his involvement in the crime.

The British Secret Intelligence Service, the plot, the torture, a slow and painful death and Rasputin's assassination

Every time I return to the study of this subject I find new inconsistencies and in many cases blatant lies are disclosed. It is impossible to say exactly what happened that night and in what sequence, who was present and who did what to whom. What we can do, however, is to use the forensic evidence that is available to build a picture of what probably happened where and when. We can use the GARF files to create a picture of the timings of events and what was, and as importantly what wasn't, seen. We can analyse timings to see whether there is any fit between what is alleged to have happened and the real truth. We can compare the two 'accepted' versions to see where there is consensus or dissent in the stories.

Unfortunately many still refuse to accept the forensic evidence that labels Purishkevich and Yusupov as liars and wish to cling to the romantic and heroic version of events. Rasputin's death was calculated, brutal, violent and slow and it was orchestrated by John Scale, Stephen Alley and Oswald Rayner through the close personal relationship that existed between Rayner and Yusupov.

We are missing a detailed (or even any) forensic examination of the interior of the Yusupov Palace, including the scene of the murder – the basement dining room, the stairways and so on – if in fact the murder did occur in the Yusupov Palace. Such an examination was not done, we are told, because Irina was a niece of the Tsar and therefore the palace could not be searched without the Tsar's authority. The inviolability of a residence of a member of the Romanov dynasty is contained in the old fundamental laws of imperial Russia. If Yusupov and Purishkevich are to be believed, the basement dining room and the stairs leading to it would have provided the equivalent of a treasure trove of forensic evidence. Surely someone asked, 'Could we look in the basement please?' How I wish we had a crime scene as gruesome as the photographs might have been so we could see the blood patterns, the state of the room, the stairs to the yard door.

Kosorotov's post mortem was conducted in the most difficult of circumstances and, while confirming to many of the 'rules' of present-day post mortems, the report is sketchy and leaves as many questions unanswered as it answers. In a modern-day PM we would have clear evidence of the bullets' track through the body, which bullets stayed in the body and which passed through, whether they were recovered or not. We would have more detailed comment on individual injuries, body temperatures and the like. Zharov and his colleagues in their re-examination of the original PM go a long way in filling the gap, as I hope does my forensic analysis throughout this book and the views of Professor Derrick Pounder.

The British involvement

It is clear from the Scale papers that he believed that Rasputin was involved in an attempt to secure a separate peace between Russia and Germany. This was a fond belief amongst those opposed to Rasputin but one for which there exists no substantial evidence. Whether it was an intelligence assessment by Scale or was fuelled by Rayner's close personal relationship with Yusupov is unclear although the latter clearly played some part in his thought process.

What are the facts? We know that at around midnight Rasputin was picked up from his flat at 64 Gorokhovaya Street. Yusupov asserts it was he who collected Rasputin and in a car driven by Dr Lazovert. Yusupov's presence is confirmed by Yekaterina Poterkina, who says she was awake at the time and saw him. This does not coincide with the description of the male who went in to collect Rasputin as given by Fyodor Korshunov. However, the description of the vehicle that collected Rasputin coincides with that described by Purishkevich – khaki and with a soft top.

We know that at some point between midnight on 16 December and 19 December, when his body was recovered from the Malaya Nevka, Rasputin was brutally murdered. We know that shots were heard that came from the direction of the Yusupov Palace between 2.30 a.m. and 4.00 a.m. on 17 December, depending on the witness account. A scream was heard by the policeman on duty across the road from the Yusupov Palace. According to Vlasyuk and Yefimov, no car was seen in the yard next to the palace or was seen leaving the palace after the shots were fired. We know that Akim Lazukov lied to Vlasyuk. Vlasyuk saw Yusupov and his butler in the yard of the palace. Sometime afterwards he was summoned to the palace, where Purishkevich told him that they had killed Rasputin. Yusupov left the palace via the front door at about 5.00 a.m.

We know the body of a dead dog was found by investigators buried under the snow in the yard of the palace. We know that blood stains were found leading from the entrance to Yusupov's private quarters to the main gate of the yard, where in a pile of snow the dog was found buried.

One of Rasputin's overshoes was recovered from the ice on the Malaya Nevka by Petrovskii Bridge at about 2.00 p.m. on 17 December and blood was found on the bridge walkway, the barrier and the fourth bridge support. Subsequently Rasputin's body was recovered from the Nevka, on 19 December, approximately 60–65 metres from the bridge, under the ice on the Petrovskii Island side. The body was wrapped in a fur coat and bound by ropes in some sort of cloth.

I believe that Yusupov, Dmitrii and Purishkevich were all present in the Yusupov Palace on the night of the murder. Rasputin had been enticed to the palace for a meeting and once in the basement dining room, a room selected because the sound of shots would be muffled, was plied with drink and discussion revolved around the war. The presence of these three men was in my view necessary to provide witness to Rasputin's death and, after the event, to portray the still fondly held view that this was some romantic plot to save Mother Russia carried out by a member of the imperial family, the heir to a fortune and a member of the Duma. Lazovert was there to pronounce life extinct at an appropriate time. Dmitrii, Yusupov and Purishkevich provided a kind of legitimacy; one can imagine the wrath of the Tsaritsa and the Tsar had this been a plot carried out solely by British agents. It had to look as if Russians had done it and had committed murder for the right reasons. The overt involvement of British intelligence would have produced serious repercussions for the relationship between Russia and Great Britain, something that the British wished to avoid at all costs.

Whoever first conceived the idea of assassinating Rasputin I am unclear about. Was it Scale, Alley and Rayner or Yusupov, Dmitrii and Purishkevich? It is fairly clear though that from the time of Yusupov and Purishkevich's first meeting things moved rapidly towards the demise of 'Dark Forces'.

There were multiple motives for killing Rasputin but to the British a separate peace between Russia and Germany would have been devastating. Rayner's obituary states that he was present in the palace at the time of the murder. While this is hearsay it was a strongly held view within his family and it was he and no one else who told his family this. We know from Yusupov that he knew of the plot and we know he was with Yusupov the morning following the murder and escorted him to the railway station. Purishkevich had approached Samuel Hoare, the head of the SIS station, about the plot; was this to gain British involvement? I think some of the truth around the events of that night are to be found in Lazovert's account but what comes through so strongly is the attempt by all to convince the reader that only those mentioned in the 'accepted version' of events were present.

At some stage Rayner enters the scene. From his relationship with Yusupov, Rayner has developed a hatred towards Rasputin and believes that he knows much about Germany's plans. Together with a not unusually drunken Rasputin, the ingredients are in place for torture and death. Is torture a flippant aside? No, a fact that is borne out by the details of the forensic examination. The injuries contained both in Kosorotov's report of the post mortem and in Zharov's re-examination are extensive and severe. The body's collision with the bridge supports when thrown into the river accounts for some of them, but others were caused while he was alive. Yusupov's account of his frenzied attack on the body after it had been dragged back into the palace, having been shot by Purishkevich, does not hold water, firstly because we know from the forensics that the whole running-away-across-the-yard episode is a massive lie, a total fabrication.

Rasputin was tortured and experienced a slow, lingering and painful death. The forensic evidence absolutely confirms my contention. I will consider the bullet wounds in detail shortly but first I want to concentrate on the torture aspect. Rasputin, I am now convinced, was confined to the basement dining room and the whole sordid event occurred within those four walls. Let me deal with the wounds. Kosorotov observed, 'His neck has a wound from some sort of rope tie.' There is no evidence from the scene-of-crime photographs of a rope tie around Rasputin's body and in any case to create such a mark the rope would have needed to have been tied very tightly against the skin, not through cloth and clothing. I believe that Rasputin was restrained by way of a garrotte around his neck. He was possibly seated at the time or spread-eagled against a wall.

'The victim's face and body carry traces of blows given by a supple but hard object,' Kosorotov went on. These are not post mortem injuries but injuries inflicted on Rasputin while alive – ante mortem.

197

Of course some could suggest that Yusupov and Purishkevich account for this in their version of events by Yusupov's frenzied attack but as previously discussed we know the events of the yard are a lie and that Constable Vlasyuk observed no blood on Yusupov's clothes, of which there would have been huge amounts had he carried out such an attack. This point is forcibly made by Zharov. He didn't notice Yusupov's torn jacket – as Rasputin's resurrection never occurred.

In crime cases where torture is involved, victims are often beaten, either for information or merely to humiliate them or cause them pain. Kosorotov goes on to say, 'His genitals have been crushed by the action of a similar object.' It is hard to believe that someone could inflict such injury, but I am afraid to a seasoned detective it is nothing unusual. I do not want to enter the realms of drama but Rasputin was debauched: he enjoyed sex with women, possibly men as well, and destroying his manhood would have a profound effect. In such a situation the conversation and progress of the torture is not difficult to envision. After a substantial beating with little intelligence gained, because he had none to give, Rasputin is threatened with an attack on his genitals. He makes no response and so he is hit with a cosh in the genitals, causing absolute agony, if not unconsciousness. Alternatively, as previously discussed, this could be a sexually provoked attack in revenge for some act he carried out, possibly with Yusupov; however, I doubt this.

'His left side has a weeping wound, due to some sort of slicing object or a sword,' Kosorotov goes on. No one mentions a sword, a knife or a razor in their recollections but the evidence is clear: this is not some amateur commentator's assessment but the words of the pathologist. Rasputin was beaten, knifed and finally shot.

At the end of his abuse the decision is made to kill him, he was hardly in any fit state to go anywhere. We will never know how

Kosorotov ascertained that the first two shots were delivered while he was standing but we know that they were fired from close range (20 centimetres), one from the left-hand side passing through the stomach and the liver, seriously damaging the left lobe, and the other from behind through the kidney. We know that these wounds were caused by two weapons of different calibres, although how Kosorotov ascertained this we do not know; maybe he had the bullets, maybe he deduced it from the size of the wounds. Yet more was to come: Rasputin's demise was made certain by a third shot delivered at point blank range to his forehead by a gun of yet another different calibre.

Professor Pounder is not given to making wild claims; his professional integrity depends on assessment of forensic evidence. Nevertheless, he is certain that the wound to Rasputin's head was caused by a .455 Webley, the standard British issue side arm in the First World War. I also concluded from my own assessment that the wound was caused by that type of weapon, while Zharov is clear that it was made by a larger-calibre weapon than the other two used. Variously we are told Dmitrii had a Browning, Yusupov a pocket Browning and Purishkevich a Savage – all automatic weapons and not bulky revolvers.

Who would have used a .455 Webley? The simple answer is Oswald Rayner, the same Rayner who was Yusupov's close friend, the man who had prior knowledge of the plot and would be in Yusupov's presence after the murder. Professor Pounder's evidence became even more compelling as he told me: 'The prominent grazing around the margins of the wound, visible in the post mortem photograph, is indicative of the marginal abrasion caused by a non-jacketed – i.e. lead – bullet and in this case one of a large calibre. The use of a lead non-jacketed bullet strongly indicates a revolver rather than a pistol.' For those who have sought to disparage the theory that the British SIS were involved and that it was Rayner who fired the fatal head shot, Pounder's evidence is damning.

The stories of bodies being dragged backwards and forwards are implausible and my assessment is that the torture, assassination and wrapping of the body all occurred in the basement room. It is the only place that has the space – can you imagine dragging the body up and down the narrow stairs or trying to wrap it up on the small landing that leads out to the yard? The reality is 'no', because it was never necessary to do these things. The yard episode never happened, as I believe I have conclusively shown. There was also more thought put into the disposal of the body than the accounts suggest; for example none of them mentions the ropes that were used to tie Rasputin's hands and legs. Were they just lying around the palace?

As I have studied the events of 16–17 December in more detail I have realised that my initial *Timewatch* assessment was wrong and this was a cynical conspiracy that lacked little in its planning and was probably based around a misjudgement of the response to Rasputin's murder by the Tsar. The whole of the events that were alleged to have taken place in the yard of 92 Moika Embankment are a ruse to support the picture of Rasputin as some supernatural hero. I asked the question earlier: would even the most inept conspirators take a body out into the yard of 92 Moika Embankment under the gaze of the police post across the road? The answer is simply no; not even Yusupov at his dilettante best would be so stupid. The farce of Rasputin's resurrection didn't occur, there was no escape into the yard, no heroes rushing here and there along the pavement abutting the yard. We know from Vlasyuk's evidence that the body wasn't in the yard. The bullet wounds and the dreadful beating, particularly the beating, would have all left blood stains, heavy blood stains on the assailants. Yet Vlasyuk notes no such stains on Yusupov or

Purishkevich, and what is more he doesn't notice that Yusupov's uniform is missing an epaulette that was supposedly torn off by Rasputin in his bid to escape.

We then have to look at the provision of the material to wrap Rasputin in and the rope, which was not mentioned previously. The disposal of the body had been subject to considerable thought: throwing the body, in a tight bundle, into a fast-flowing river close to the Gulf of Finland would see it gone forever. This occurred at or before 2.30 a.m. Rasputin's body was removed through what most people would call the rear of the Moika palace, a large but secluded courtyard accessed by a long driveway with a porter's lodge and gates where it joined the road, away from the view of the police. The conspirators were not stupid enough, whatever many might think, to play this tragedy out right under the noses of the police. We know from the police witnesses that no cars stopped at the front of the palace after the shots were fired, and no one was seen moving a body backwards and forwards. There was never any body in the yard of No. 92. No; Rasputin's corpse was removed precisely and out of sight of the authorities and taken by car from the rear entrance to Petrovskii Bridge.

Rob Monash has kindly supplied me with some photographs of the palace (Plates 19 and 20), which show the courtyard area, the drive leading to it and the substantial gated porter's lodge where the palace property meets the public highway, which at the time was called Ofitserskaya Street.

The body was driven to Petrovskii Bridge, where it was thrown into the large ice hole. On the way down it bounced off the fourth bridge support, which may account for some of the injuries to the right side of Rasputin's head, and his overshoe landed up on the ice. Neither Purishkevich nor Dmitrii travelled in the car, but in all probability enjoyed a celebration of Rasputin's death at the Yusupov Palace. I would suggest that Lazovert (the driver), Sergei Sukhotin, Ivan Nefedov and one or more British agents travelled in the car to the bridge and disposed of the body. It was Sukhotin who had originally discovered the ice hole, according to one of the accounts.

Meanwhile back at the Yusupov Palace, concerns had started to emerge, maybe prompted by a third party, that the shots there might have been heard – as in fact they were, by Lazukov and Bobkov, the Yusupovs' two employees. They therefore decided to shoot one of the palace dogs, which we know was discovered. The shots Vlasyuk and Yefimov heard were the ones that killed the dog and the scream was the cry of the dog as it was shot (I have heard this scream or howl before). One shot should kill a dog. Of course it is strange that no one heard these shots, if you accept Yusupov's version of events. Here were the police on high alert having heard shots before and then they failed to hear a dog being shot in the yard – inconceivable!

The dog was laid on the snow and we know that despite Yusupov telling Vlasyuk that a dog had been shot, the policeman was not shown the corpse. Nefedov told the police that he carried the dead dog from the yard of 92 Moika Embankment to the Yusupov Palace gardens, which are at the rear of the palace. This accounts for the blood trail from the gates of the yard to the side door. It also accounts for Yusupov being so calm and composed when he spoke to Vlasyuk in the yard. There was no body there; it had been taken away before the police even became aware of the shots. Furthermore, it explains why there was no blood on Yusupov when Vlasyuk appeared in the study.

This was not a bungled murder. It was well planned, from the muffling effect of the basement room to a very clinical close-range *coup de grâce*, to disposing of the body where it was intended that it should float out into the Gulf of Finland, never to be recovered. All that went wrong was the shots that killed the dog and the boot and overshoe being dislodged as the body fell into the Nevka. The final error was not to have gauged the flow of the Malaya Nevka to the Gulf of Finland.

We may never know exactly what happened in the basement of 94 Moika Embankment during the early hours of 17 December, but what we do know is that the accepted versions from Purishkevich and Yusupov are a tissue of lies and that Radzinskii's proposal that Dmitrii was the murderer is not supportable.

*

In English law perversion of the course of justice is a criminal offence in which someone acts in a manner that in some way prevents justice being served on either themselves or on a third party. It is an offence in common law and carries a theoretical maximum sentence of life imprisonment. Perversion of the course of justice takes the form of one of three acts: fabrication or disposal of evidence, intimidating a witness or juror, or threatening a witness or juror. Conspiracy, meanwhile, is an agreement between two or more persons to break the law at some time in the future, and, in some cases, with at least one overt act in furtherance of that agreement. I suggest that Purishkevich, Yusupov and Lazovert together with others were guilty of a conspiracy to pervert the course of justice, in this case to fabricate evidence. We know that Yusupov, Purishkevich and Lazovert lied in their accounts so much so that I feel able to say in most aspects they are a total fabrication. But it is very unusual to pervert the course of justice by taking the blame upon oneself; how did this happen?

I suppose what has compelled people to accept the 'accepted versions' of events over the years has been the almost spontaneous way in which the story emerged, literally the day after the murder and circulated by Yusupov. However, it was Purishkevich that first went to print, but why did he lie? The complexity of the conspirators' account is stunning but it falls apart on closer analysis. The pre-planning to have a story to tell the day after the murder was substantial and I would guess it was done on the basis of 'if anything goes wrong', which we know it did: gunshots were heard and the body became trapped under the ice rather than sinking to the river bed or floating out into the Baltic never to be seen again. There was no way the real story, that the British SIS were involved, could come out so Dmitrii, Yusupov and Purishkevich were all necessary to provide a sense of respectability around the murder and to make it a romantic 'saving Mother Russia' affair. Dmitrii needed to be involved to provide the legal protection surrounding a grand duke and so, whether tutored by the British or by their own resolve, they set about fabricating a story that was both compelling and heroic. For nearly ninety years they got away with it until their accounts were dismantled, the forensics examined and evidence of the SIS involvement emerged. The Tsar had no doubt of Rayner's involvement on the night.

It is most unfortunate for us that prior to his death Oswald Rayner destroyed all his files. A guilty conscience, or details of a heinous crime that brought little credit on those involved? We will never know.

There is one piece of controversial but damning post-murder evidence which I accept, after exhaustive examination, as being genuine, and that is a letter sent by Alley to Scale. In the *Timewatch* programme, I am shown in the lounge area of the Astoria Hotel considering a letter, which had only been handed to me minutes before, that purports to have been written by Stephen Alley to John Scale on 7 January 1917. The letter, at face value, in my opinion conclusively shows the involvement of Scale, Alley and Rayner in the murder of Rasputin. My opportunity, at that time, to assess the letter in detail was minimal and its authenticity has been called into doubt by many commentators on the Alexander Palace Discussion Forum.

The letter was recovered from distant relatives of Alley living in South Africa by researchers for the programme. In the top left hand corner it shows the address:

British Intelligence Mission
Attached
Head Quarters
Russian Imperial Grand Staff
Petrograd

This heading appears on numerous other official letters created by SIS officers during the period and therefore appears genuine. However, on the Alley–Scale letter it is set slightly higher up the page than on the other letters, although this could be as a result of it coming from a different printing run. Much controversy has also been raised over the appearance of the date on the letter. The key issue is that the figure 1 in '1917' is typed as on modern typefaces, but at the time and for many years afterwards many typewriters used a lower-case L to denote the figure 1. To some this discredited the letter immediately. However, I made enquiries of Paul Robert of the Virtual Typewriter Museum, who provided me with the following information:

What I can tell by the script on this letter is that this letter was typed on what was at the time a fairly standard typewriter . . . The machine was also well used and needed maintenance, because the adjustment was off. The person who operated the machine was an experienced but somewhat sloppy typist. The font looks like a standard 9-pitch pica. So, yes, the only thing that is slightly odd about it is the fact that the machine had a separate key for the 1.

. . . This was less uncommon than you may think. As early as 1892 there was a separate 1 key on the Empire typewriter (Canadian machine), which was also built in Germany as the Adler 7. In England, the 1 appeared on the 1908 Imperial typewriter, which was produced in Leicester. I know that both machines were bought in numbers by the British government. If I had to choose between the two, I would guess that the machine used here was an Imperial, because the Empire in general had much better adjustment than the Imperial.

Therefore it is highly feasible that Alley was using a typewriter which had the figure 1 on its keyboard. I have looked at other letters produced from the same office, during the same period, and none of those display the figure 1 but use a lower-case L. However, it is probable that in the office there were several typewriters.

I then had my attention drawn to Alley's signature on the letter and I was shown letters that were signed by him dated 24 October 1922 and 19 June 1917. These two letters have a flamboyant signature that is replicated on other pieces of his correspondence. Analysis of these signatures establishes beyond doubt that they were not produced by the same person who signed the letter to Scale, in a very plain style, as Stephen Alley. It would have been easy for me at this stage to suggest that the letter was not genuine. However, further review of Alley's letters shows that the letter of 19 June bears two signatures, Alley's genuine flamboyant one and at the side another, 'Stephen Alley'. This second signature is again plain and analysis shows that it was not written by the person who produced the flamboyant one, nor was it produced by whoever signed the Alley–Scale letter on 7 January 1917. To me this suggests that staff within the SIS office would sign letters on behalf of others rather than use the accepted convention of signing their own names *per pro* the author.

Questions have also been raised about why Alley should write such a letter and how it would reach Scale. The days of mobile phones were many decades away, of course, and communication was generally either by telegram or letter so a letter is a reasonable way to communicate, sent either by courier or by normal military despatches.

In the absence of evidence to the contrary the letter has to be accepted as genuine or else – and the spectre of this concerns me – created ex post facto for the purpose of financial gain, a view which I do not accept and in the absence of proof reject. I have seen criticism of the content of the letter that suggests it does not conclusively show British involvement, the logic of which eludes me. Let me dissect it.

'Dear Scale, No response has thus far been received from London in respect of your oilfields proposal.' There is clear evidence to show Scale's involvement in the destruction of the Romanian oil fields in face of the advancing German troops.

'Although matters have not proceeded entirely to plan, our objective has clearly been achieved.' Well, we know things had not gone to plan: the body had been recovered from the Nevka when the intention was that it would never be seen again; Yusupov had been detained at the station on the way to the Crimea; the police had attended the Yusupov Palace as a result of hearing 'shots'. But if the objective was, as I suggest, to prevent a separate peace with Germany by removing Rasputin, then yes, it had been achieved.

'Reaction to the demise of "Dark Forces" has been well received by all, although a few awkward questions have already been asked about wider involvement.' We know that Purishkevich referred to Rasputin as 'Dark Forces', and we know from the Scale papers and from his daughter's evidence that her father used the same term when referring to Rasputin – this was the accepted code word for him. This issue is not in doubt and William Le Queux used the term 'Dark Forces' to describe Rasputin as early as 1918.[3] Brian Moynahan provides more information about how commonly the term was applied to Rasputin when he tells us:

On December 8 the Union of Towns, an important municipal body, went into secret session. It passed a resolution: 'The government, now become an instrument of the dark forces, is driving Russia to her ruin and is shattering the imperial throne. In this grave hour the country requires a government worthy of a great people. There is not a day to lose!' Secrets were no longer kept. The resolution was circulated in Roneo script in thousands of copies. 'Dark forces' was simple code for Grigorii Rasputin and those about him.[4]

And I hope no one would doubt he died and therefore it was his 'demise'. We know that awkward questions had been asked: the Tsar confronted the British ambassador and accused Rayner (although not by name) of being involved. Hoare had become involved in the debate and there were some very tricky questions to be answered.

Alley's letter goes on: 'Rayner is attending to loose ends and will no doubt brief you on your return.' We know that Rayner was with Yusupov the morning after the murder, and we also know he was with Yusupov at the station when Yusupov was arrested.

It is very difficult to see how anyone, given the analysis of the letter and the facts I have outlined above, cannot say that it provides primary evidence of British involvement and that the 'accepted version' of the events was in fact a cynical conspiracy to pervert the course of justice.

CONCLUSION

Looking at all the evidence we have before us, a clear picture emerges of what happened. On the night of 16–17 December 1916 Rasputin was lured using some pretence to the Yusupov Palace on the Moika. He was collected in a car and driven to the palace. His arrival was not witnessed by anyone not party to the conspiracy to murder him. He was taken to the basement dining room, which the conspirators had selected because it was below street level and only had small windows and therefore the sound of shots would be muffled. Almost certainly Feliks Yusupov, Vladimir Purishkevich and Grand Duke Dmitrii were present to witness his demise and had been party to the conspiracy to lure him to the palace. Dr Stanislaus de Lazovert was probably there for the sole purpose of pronouncing 'life extinct'. Rasputin almost certainly thought he was visiting the palace for a social event and it is probable that the early part of what was to become an ordeal for Rasputin started in a convivial atmosphere.

Oswald Rayner, a member of the British Secret Intelligence Service, his boss, John Scale, and those present that night wrongly believed Rasputin was petitioning for a separate peace with Germany. It is almost certain that Yusupov and his fellow conspirators questioned him gently at first about what he knew of German intentions. It is doubtful that their information-gathering exercise provided any fruit as the intelligence on which their questions were based was flawed. Frustrated by the lack of any meaningful response from Rasputin their mood, and the mood of the evening, were to change and it is probable that those assembled were joined early on by Oswald Rayner and possibly others. Rayner's business was intelligence and intelligence he was going to have.

Feelings were intense that night. Purishkevich had spoken openly in the Duma of his absolute dislike of Rasputin, and Dmitrii would have hated the scandal that had befallen the Tsar and Tsaritsa as a result of their relationship with the *starets*. Yusupov's motivation is less clear but it is undoubtedly the case that he encouraged the SIS belief that Rasputin was pro-German.

All the evidence suggests that he was not poisoned using cyanide, as the 'accepted version' of his death claims, but he had been drinking heavily. He was seized upon and bound, and a rope was placed around his neck, the purpose being to extract by torture details of his dealings with pro-German elements. He was assaulted with a cosh, and probably also fists and a sharp implement, and as a final indignity his genitals were crushed with the self-same cosh.

The beating continued as, in immense pain and bleeding profusely, Rasputin failed to provide Rayner with any meaningful information, simply because we now know he didn't have that information to give. It is probable that despite gaining no intelligence the conspirators decided to kill him, which had been the original intention, but there was less resonance now as without any confession Rasputin could not be legitimately branded a traitor. The sentence of the conspirators was death by shooting; who fired the first two shots we may never know. The first shot was to Rasputin's left side and travelled in an upward trajectory through the stomach and liver, shattering its lobe. The second, fired shortly afterwards, was to the right-hand side of his back and penetrated the kidney, damaging it massively. Rasputin if conscious would almost certainly have known who fired the shots as they were both fired from within 20 centimetres. But Oswald Rayner walked up to Rasputin, dying or already dead, placed his revolver against Rasputin's forehead and pulled the trigger.

The forensic evidence tells us there was no dramatic resurrection and attempted escape after the first shot, no chase across the yard of 92 Moika Embankment, no Purishkevich firing at him from 20 metres and dropping him with two precisely aimed shots. Therefore there was no body to be seen in the yard, and no cars leaving and returning to the Moika side of the palace.

The conspirators planned well: a doctor on hand to certify death, all the materials they needed to wrap Rasputin's body in a shroud and bind his legs and arms with rope. A car was waiting at the rear of the palace, out of the gaze of the police, to convey the body swiftly to Petrovskii Bridge on the Malaya Nevka, where gaps in the ice had been identified. Rasputin's body, with his beaver coat wrapped around it, was tipped over the bridge rails, bounced off the bridge supports and disappeared into the cold, dark waters of the largely ice-covered, fast-flowing river, hopefully never to be seen again, taken by the current to the Baltic Sea. Rasputin did not, despite the popular myth, enter the water alive and attempt to loose his bonds in a desperate bid to free himself; he died in the Yusupov Palace. This was no amateur assassination. It was cynical, cold and calculated even to the extent that a cover story was prepared and agreed by the conspirators.

The life of 'Dark Forces' and the whole shameful episode of his torture and demise ended when Oswald Rayner pulled the trigger of his .455 British Army standard issue revolver, delivering the *coup de grâce* to the forehead in a shot which was immediately fatal.

KOSOROTOV'S POST MORTEM REPORT

I, Professor Kosorotov, declare that I have been to the autopsy of Rasputin's dead body, on 20 December 1916 at ten o'clock in the evening, in the mortuary room of Chesmenskii Hospice. The body was recognised by his two daughters, his niece, his secretary and various witnesses.

The body is that of a man of about fifty years old, of medium size, dressed in a blue embroidered hospital robe, which covers a white shirt. His legs, in tall animal skin boots, are tied with a rope, and the same rope ties his wrists. His dishevelled hair is light brown, as are his long moustache and beard, and it's soaked with blood. His mouth is half open, his teeth clenched. His face below his forehead is covered in blood. His shirt too is also marked with blood.

There are three bullet wounds. The first has penetrated the left side of the chest and has gone through the stomach and the liver. The second has entered into the right side of the back and gone through the kidney. This is a similar wound to the one on the left side and is also caused by a firearm being fired at close range. The third has hit the victim on the forehead and penetrated into his brain.

Bullet analysis
The first two bullets hit the victim standing. The third bullet hit the victim while he was lying on the ground. The bullets came from different calibre revolvers.

Examination of the head

The cerebral matter gave off a strong smell of alcohol.

Examination of the stomach

The stomach contains about twenty soup spoons of liquid smelling of alcohol. The examination reveals no trace of poison.

Wounds

His left side has a weeping wound, due to some sort of slicing object or a sword. His right eye has come out of its cavity and falls down onto his face. At the corner of the right eye the membrane is torn. His right ear is hanging down and torn. His neck has a wound from some sort of rope tie. The victim's face and body carry traces of blows given by a supple but hard object. His genitals have been crushed by the action of a similar object.

Causes of death

Haemorrhage caused by a wound to the liver and the wound to the right kidney must have started the rapid decline of his strength. In this case, he would have died in ten or twenty minutes. At the moment of death the deceased was in a state of drunkenness. The first bullet passed through the stomach and the liver. This mortal blow had been shot from a distance of 20 centimetres. The wound on the right side, made at nearly exactly the same time as the first, was also mortal; it passed through the right kidney. The victim, at the time of the murder, was standing. When he was shot in the forehead, his body was already on the ground.

THE OPINION OF THE SPECIALISTS

Following the request of the Moscow correspondent of the [illegible] agency, we the undersigned:

- Vladimir Vasil'yevich Zharov, head of the Forensic Medical Analysis Bureau, with a PhD in medicine, who has worked in this capacity for twenty-nine years, has the highest qualification degree and is a professor of medicine
- Igor Yevgen'yevich Panov (PhD in medicine), deputy head of the same bureau, a specialist in forensic medicine, having a 34-year experience of working in this field
- Valerii Konstantinovich Vasil'yevskii, deputy head of the same bureau, a specialist in forensic medicine with twenty-two years of experience and the highest qualification degree

have studied the photocopies of the documents of the murder of Grigorii Yefimovich Rasputin (Novykh), born in 1872, with the purpose of providing a forensic expertise of the physical injuries and the cause of death of the above, as described in the memoirs of F. F. Yusupov and V. M. Purishkevich.

The autopsy was carried out by the professor of forensic medicine from the Military Medical Academy, D. P. Kosorotov, with the help of several police doctors. The autopsy lasted till 1 a.m. The body was examined thoroughly for two hours. Apart from two gunshot wounds there were a lot of bruises. There was a lot of thick brown liquid in the stomach, but it was impossible to analyse it, because the autopsy was stopped on the orders of the Empress Alexandra Fyodorovna.

Prof. Kosorotov writes that on 19 December he got a letter from the coroner with the invitation to be present at Rasputin's autopsy on 21 December in the morning at Chesmenskii Hospice. But then under some special order, on 20 December at 7 p.m. Kosorotov was called in together with the prosecutor and the investigator to carry out the autopsy.

The autopsy showed up numerous injuries to the body, many of which Rasputin suffered posthumously. The entire right part of his head was smashed as a result of him being thrown off the bridge. Death was caused by an internal haemorrhage as a result of a gunshot wound in his stomach. He was shot at close range, according to Kosorotov, from left to right, through the stomach, into the liver, the left part of which was shattered. There was another gunshot wound on the back, in the region of the spine, and the right kidney was shattered. One more gunshot was fired into the forehead from close range, most likely when the victim was already dead or dying. The chest wounds were clean cut, not messy, and were examined superficially. No signs of drowning were found: there was no water in the respiratory organs, the lungs were not swollen. Rasputin was thrown into the water when he was already dead.

The autopsy was carried out in very poor conditions. The source of light was oil lamps. In order to examine the insides of the chest and stomach the oil lamp had to be brought into the cavity. The huge wound on the head was too upsetting for the professor. He was surprised how much they were rushed by the authorities to finish the autopsy. He wanted to be thorough and methodical.

According to Kosorotov, Rasputin was killed by a gunshot. Other gunshots were fired from close range; the bullets went right through the body. Because of that it was impossible to say how many people were shooting.

Rasputin was a robust man of forty-five years. In the opinion of the medics carrying out the autopsy he could have lived another forty-five. He was drunk at the moment of his death. There was a strong smell of whisky on his breath. His brain was of normal size; there were no pathological signs of any sort in it.

In March 1917 the preliminary investigation of Rasputin's murder was closed, and its materials were allegedly destroyed.

Analysis of the photo documents

There are thirty-three photographs and twenty slides which can be divided into the following groups:

1. Rasputin when he was alive. Six photos from different publications at different time of his life.
2. Seven photos of Yusupov's palace, of part of the courtyard and the railing along Moika Embankment.
3. Eight photos showing Petrovskii Bridge, one of the supporting bridge pylons, the ice hole and the body.
4. Ten photos of the body without clothes and two in clothes, taken in some room.

So the photos which we studied were those of Rasputin alive, of the scene of the crime, of the place where the body was found, and of the body when it was discovered and when it was first examined. It is obvious that the photos in groups 2–4 were taken by the investigators. They were taken, by and large, according to the rules of forensic photography.

Photographs of the crime scene

These photos are the general and 'orientational' photos of different parts of the crime scene. They show from two different angles and in different sizes images of part of the wall of a three-storey house, part of the courtyard and the railing. In the wall of the house there is a closed door with one [illegible]. The railing consists of seven segments; then we see the closed gates and then another four segments of the railing.

There is another gate, both parts of which are open onto the courtyard. Near the gate there is a little shed. On the cornice of one of the [illegible] one could clearly see snow. The snow in front of the door and in the courtyard had been cleared away and stored along the railing. If we assume that the door is 2.0–2.2 metres high then the distance from it to the distant open gate is 15–20 metres.

On one of the shots there is a dotted line. It starts on the threshold of the door and goes to the railing, at an angle of 40–45 degrees. It reaches a small snowdrift and then continues as a concave/convex line of approximately 10 metres. Then it bends at nearly 90 degrees towards the gate which is nearest to the house, and then, before it actually gets to that gate, it bends again, at a right angle, and continues along the railing, gradually disappearing. The dotted line seemed to have been created artificially, so as to stand out on the snow. It consists of short dashes, with the same distance between them. There are 68–70 such dashes.

Photographs of the place where the body was found

This group of photographs consists of some 'general', 'orientational' and 'key' shots. There is a photo of Petrovskii Bridge with some people on it. In one of the photos there is a bridge pylon, on which blood was discovered in three places. Unfortunately, there is no scale. If we assume that the height of the people on the bridge is 1.6–1.7 metres then the distance from the railing of the bridge to the pylon on which the blood was discovered is approximately 4 metres. The blood stains on the pylon are encircled with a dotted line. Only in one place could one clearly see that the stains have an irregular rectangular or oval shape of 20 × 25 × 10 centimetres and an irregular triangular shape of 10 × 10 centimetres. Our attention was drawn to the fact that the blood stains on the upper beam of the pylon are exactly above the stains on the lower beam.

A key photograph of the part of the river [shows] pieces of ice of different sizes and an ice hole. Near the edge of the ice hole there are ten or eleven boards with the body of a man lying between them. Closer to the shore, at some distance from the feet of the body, there is a dark object. It is shorter than the body. The object is covered with ice; it resembles in its shape a fur coat.

On the 'key photo', one can see that the body (the beard is clearly visible) is lying on its back, face up. The arms are raised to shoulder level and the elbows are bent. The hands are lying at the level of the head at some distance from each other. The right hand is higher than the left one. The fingers of the right hand are bent, the nails of the fingers resting on the surface of the thumb. The fingers of the left hand are in a similar position, but they are more clenched. Around the right wrist there is a loop of a rope, and there is a knot with several ends on the forearm. On the left wrist one could not see a rope. There is a white shirt on the body. It is pleated on the chest. The lower end of the shirt is level with the middle of the chest. Underneath this shirt there is an undershirt. Its hem is tucked into the trousers at the front, but at the back it is not tucked in, and is rolled up as high as the middle of the spine. The lower part of the body is wrapped up in a dark cloth. There is an indentation in the cloth in the region of the shins, suggesting that this part of the body is tied up. Between the waist and the feet one could see about seven coils of the rope. The knees are bent.

[Another] 'key photograph' shows the head and the upper part of the body. The eyelids of the right eye are open unnaturally wide although because of the wrong angle [from which the photograph was taken], and because of some mud and ice, we could not give our opinion on it.

Photographs of the first external examination of the body
The photos of this group have much better images; the body was washed and, as a result, the injuries are more visible.

On the back of the body there are some putrid spots and also some light-coloured spots caused by the pressure of the clothing on the body. There is a putrid venous web. There are some signs suggesting a deep cut wound on the back of the right shoulder and the upper third of the upper arm. But after a closer look on the enlarged image, it is obvious from its shape and the shape of its edges that this is not an injury.

Despite the posthumous changes and some facial injuries there is no doubt that the body is that of G. Y. Rasputin. The microscopic study of Rasputin's photographs and the photographs of the dead body proves that it is the same person. The shape of the eyebrows, ears and moustache and the very characteristic shape of the wings of the nose do not leave any doubt that this is the body of Rasputin.

After the study of the photos the following injuries were detected: in the middle of the forehead and somewhat higher than mid-distance between the hair line and the bridge of the nose, there is evidence of a gunshot wound (let's call it injury no. 1). This wound is of an irregular shape: its right edge is arch-like and the left one is drawn in. One could not identify the size of it . . . the iris of the eyes is clearly visible. Its size is 0.95 centimetres. Judging from its size, it is not difficult to determine the height of the forehead (the distance between the hair line and the bridge of the nose) and that the size of the wound is approx. 0.5 × 0.4 centimetres. Approximately 0.2 centimetres away from the right lower edge of the wound, there is a dark semicircle 0.15–0.20 centimetres wide. It could be a mark left by the muzzle of a gun, the so-called 'standsmark'.

In the region of the upper right part of the pubis there is an oval mark of 1.3 × 0.6 centimetres, which can be a bruise. There is a similar mark in the middle of the hair line.

The white of the right eye is very dark, suggesting a haemorrhage of the retina.

In the region of the inner corner of the right eye, lower eye-lid, upper and outside part of the right jaw there is an S-shaped injury. It seems to be a bruise with the epicentre in the corner of the eye. Underneath it, in the middle of the right cheek, there are two scratches, one circular, approx. 0.5 × 0.5 centimetres, the other oval, 1.2 × 0.5 centimetres.

The nose looks a little squashed and deformed, compared to the photo of Rasputin alive, especially the tip and the bridge. On the bridge of the nose, on the front and right part of it there are numerous scratches of irregular shape.

There is a Γ-shaped scratch on the right jaw. The right side of the forehead is bruised. Here, 2.5–3 centimetres above the outer corner of the right eye and 3–4 centimetres behind it – there are two scratches of irregular shape, approximately 1 × 1 centimetre and 0.8 × 0.8 centimetres.

In the region of the right ear and right temple there seem to be a lot of scratches and haemorrhages. But it is impossible to identify their character, shape and size, due to the technical defects of the photos.

On the left side of the chest – equidistant between the left nipple and the rib curve – there is a wound of nearly oval shape, with injured skin around it (injury no. 2). The edges of the wound are jagged. The diameter of the wound is approximately two times bigger than the head of the match visible on the photo, which is about 0.3 centimetres. The diameter of the wound is approx. 1.2 times smaller than the diameter of the nipple, which is normally 0.6–0.7 centimetres. Thus the diameter of the wound is about 0.55–0.60 centimetres. Round the wound the colour of the skin is darker, especially towards the back of the body.

On the surface of the right side of the chest, at the level of the armpit, equidistant between the imaginary lines from the nipple and the navel drawn perpendicular to the long axis of the body, there is a wound of an irregular oval shape with small protuberances of irregular star shape (injury no. 3). Using the sizes of the head of the match and the nipple, one could determine the size of this wound; it is approximately 1.0 × 0.8 centimetres. Around this wound the skin is also darker, but less so than around the wound on the left.

On the back of the body in the lumbar region there is a wound of an irregular shape, the diameter of which is 1.5 times bigger than that of the head of the match (injury no. 4). One can assume that the diameter of this wound is about 0.45–0.50 centimetres. The edges of the wound cannot be seen clearly. The skin around it has got normal colouration. There is also a wound with sharp and even edges approx. 2.7 centimetres long on the back of the body to the left of the spine. It is at 30 degrees to the vertical axis of the body (injury No 5). It is a gaping wound. There is some discolouration of the skin next to the outer left edge of the wound.

There are no other injuries identified by us on the body.

Analysis of the facts

From the above materials it is clear that on the night of 17 December 1916, over 20–30 minutes Rasputin took a lethal dose of potassium cyanide, together with the cakes and the wine. We should emphasise that taking potassium cyanide together with wine should have speeded up the effect of the poison, because in acidic conditions potassium cyanide turns into hydrocyanic acid, which causes poisoning. But in this case poisoning did not cause death. Rasputin felt unwell, was breathing heavily and was complaining of having a heavy head and some burning in the stomach. During the autopsy, Prof. Kosorotov, one of the leading specialists in forensic medicine of the time, did not record the characteristic almond smell of the internal organs, specific to the cyanide compounds.

If potassium cyanide was indeed put into the cakes and wine, then poisoning did not occur due to one of the following two factors:

1. The potassium cyanide used had been stored too long and turned into potash (K_2CO_3) and lost its toxic properties.
2. The cakes had sugar in them, which contains glucose ($C_6H_{12}O_6$). In 1888 Heinrich Kiliani, chemist and PhD at Munich University, the pupil of E. Erlenmeyer, showed that glucose and fructose become a compound with hydrogen cyanide and form the harmless cyanhydrin.

Later on, the German Nobel laureate in organic chemistry E. Fischer elaborated on this in his research into the enlarging of the hydrogen chain. So if one takes a lethal dose of potassium cyanide together with a lot of carbohydrates, poisoning may not occur.

At the same time cyanic acid is a very strong poison, which in the first place affects the medulla. It stimulates the breathing at the beginning and then inhibits it. If a dose is small, a poisoned person gets a headache, an unpleasant sensation in the mouth and a very dry tingling throat and his voice becomes coarse. One may be short of breath, and have convulsions and bulging eyes. Yusupov saw all these signs in Rasputin, which means that a small dose unable to cause lethal poisoning affected Rasputin after all.

From the memoirs of Yusupov and Purishkevich, it is clear that Yusupov shot Rasputin from his Browning once – the bullet going into the chest in the heart region and coming out again. Purishkevich fired four times. He missed twice, the third bullet hit Rasputin in the back, the fourth one in the head. Yusupov was shooting at close range, Purishkevich from a distance of 20 yards.

According to Prof. Kosorotov, there were three gunshot wounds on the body. One of them, the chest one, damaged the stomach and the liver, the bullet going in and out of the body. The other one, in the back, caused damage to the right kidney, and according to Kosorotov, once more the bullet went clean through. A third bullet, from the wound in the forehead, was extracted by the forensic medics.

Having studied the photos we arrived at the conclusion that the wounds in the region of the chest to the left (injury no. 2) and to the right (injury no. 3), in the region of the forehead (injury no. 1) and in the back (injury no. 4) are of gunshot origin. After comparing the size, shape and character of the edges of these wounds [we can say] they are gunshot bullet wounds, while injury no. 3 is the wound where the bullet came out. So Prof. Kosorotov's opinion, which we support, is that the bullet in the back stayed in the body, while the bullet in the chest went through. As a result we conclude that the shot to the chest was fired at close range (there appears to be a round 'standsmark' on the wound from the muzzle of the gun). Prof. Kosorotov does not mention in his report the bullet coming out of the head and there are no images of the back of the head on the photographs.

We do not have the data to establish the calibre of the weapon with which Rasputin was shot. We can only assume that the chest wound was caused by a 6.35mm gun or smaller. It could be, for example, a Browning No. 3 1906 model, a 'Baby' Browning or a Mauser 1910 model.

Wounds to the stomach and liver tend to cause shock and internal haemorrhaging. The wounded normally cannot move or be active. But sometimes a very fit person, especially under the moderate influence of alcohol, in extreme life-threatening circumstances, can actually walk or even run for a while, put up resistance and so on. So the actions of Rasputin, after he had been wounded in the stomach, as described by Yusupov and Purishkevich, could indeed have taken place.

As the forensic medicine shows, the bullet wounds in the head shot from close range caused severe destruction of the brain matter. Normally, immediately after a wound of such nature, there is a loss of consciousness and, as a result, an inability to perform any actions. The time it takes before the onset of death depends on which part of the brain is damaged and how badly. There is no mention of this on Prof. Kosorotov's report.

We agree with Prof. Kosorotov's opinion that the cause of death was not drowning and Rasputin was already dead when he was thrown into the water. Indeed Kosorotov confirms his opinion with some evidence (the lungs were not swollen and there was no water in the respiratory organs).

The question whether the bruises on the face were inflicted before or after Rasputin's death is impossible to answer, due to the lack of information. These injuries were caused by heavy, blunt objects. Rasputin was definitely hit more than once. Some injuries were inflicted when the body was thrown off the bridge. The presence of blood on the pylon of Petrovskii Bridge proves this. It is possible that the injuries on the face were caused by the blows of the rubber cane or weight, and the person who inflicted these injuries had his clothes covered in blood. The cut on the left side of the back (injury no. 5) was caused by a sharp object used only once (knife, razor etc). It is impossible to say whether this wound was inflicted before or after death.

Conclusion

It is possible that the lethal dose of potassium cyanide did not cause Rasputin's death. The poisoning did not occur, either as a result of cyanide changing its chemical status . . . [text illegible] The nature of Rasputin's complaints about feeling unwell after he took the poisoned cakes and wine are characteristic of light poisoning.

The autopsy of Rasputin showed three gunshot wounds where the bullets remained in the body and one wound where the bullet came out; one cut; and many bruises on the head caused by a heavy, blunt object. It is impossible to determine the type or the calibre of the gun from which he was shot (pistol or revolver), but we can assume that it was a 6.35mm weapon.

It is also impossible to conclude the sequence, and the distance from which the shots were fired. We can only suppose that out of three gunshots, the one to the head was the last. This shot shows all the signs of being fired at close range. The shot into the chest was probably fired at quite a close distance as well.

The mechanical injuries (the ones not caused by gunshots) in the region of the head were caused by a succession of blows inflicted by heavy, blunt objects. These injuries could not have been caused by the body hitting the pylon of the bridge from which it was thrown off.

The cut on the back was caused by a sharp object, possibly a knife or a razor blade. It is not possible to say whether this injury happened before or after death.

After Rasputin was wounded in his stomach and liver, it is possible that he could walk, run and put up resistance for the next 5–15 minutes.

After he was wounded in the head, it is dubious that he was able to act with purpose and co-ordination.

The injury most likely to have caused the death is the shot in the head, which caused damage to the brain matter.

There was no evidence of drowning in the studied materials.

Moscow, 18–30 June 1993

NOTES

Preface

1. Radzinsky, E. (2000), *Rasputin: The Last Word*, tr. J. Rosengrant, London: Weidenfeld & Nicolson.
2. King, G. and Wilson, P. (2003), *The Fate of the Romanovs*, Hoboken, NJ: John Wiley & Sons.

Introduction

1. Paléologue, M. (1925), *An Ambassador's Memoirs*, vol. 3, tr. F. Holt, London: Hutchinson.
2. Le Queux, W. (1918), *The Minister of Evil: The Secret History of Rasputin's Betrayal of Russia*, London: Cassell.

Chapter 1: The main players

1. Figes, O. (1996), *A People's Tragedy: The Russian Revolution 1891–1924*, London: Jonathan Cape.
2. Youssoupoff, F. (1953), *Lost Splendour*, tr. A. Green and N. Katkoff, London: Jonathan Cape.
3. Davidson, L., 'Grand Duke Dimitry Pavlovich', Alexander Palace website.
4. Shishkin, O. (2000), *Ubit' Rasputina*, Moscow: Olma-Press.
5. Yusupov, F. (1927), *Rasputin: His Malignant Influence and His Assassination*, tr. O. Rayner, London: Jonathan Cape.

Chapter 2: Prelude to murder

1. Purishkevich, V. M. (1984), *The Murder of Rasputin*, ed. and tr. M. E. Shaw, Ann Arbor, MI: Ardis.

Chapter 3: Some reported versions of Rasputin's murder

1. Yusupov, F. (1927), *Rasputin: His Malignant Influence and His Assassination*, tr. O. Rayner, London: Jonathan Cape.

2. Youssoupoff, F. (1953), *Lost Splendour*, tr. A. Green and N. Katkoff, London: Jonathan Cape; Youssoupoff, F. (2003), *Lost Splendor: The Amazing Memoirs of the Man Who Killed Rasputin*, tr. A. Green and N. Katkoff, New York: Helen Marx. Available on the Alexander Palace website.
3. Purishkevich, V. M. (1984), *The Murder of Rasputin*, ed. and tr. M. E. Shaw, Ann Arbor, MI: Ardis.
4. Horne, C. F. and Austin, W. F. (eds) (1923), *Source Records of the Great War*, vol. V, US National Alumni.
5. Paléologue, M. (1923–5), *An Ambassador's Memoirs*, 3 vols, tr. F. Holt, London: Hutchinson. Available on the Alexander Palace website.
6. Buxhoeveden, S. (1928), *The Life and Tragedy of Alexandra Feodorovna, Empress of Russia*, London: Longmans. Available on the Alexander Palace website.
7. Stopford, A. (1919), *Russian Diary of an Englishman: Petrograd 1915–1917*, London: William Heinemann.

Chapter 4: Motives

1. See Maylunas, A. (1996), *A Lifelong Passion: Nicholas and Alexandra – Their Own Story*, London: Weidenfeld & Nicolson.
2. A. P. and D. A. Kotsyubinskii (2003), *Grigorii Rasputin: tainyi i yavnyi*, St Petersburg: Limbus Press.

Chapter 5: The primary crime scene

1. GARF files.
2. Batten, J. (1995), *Mind over Murder: DNA and Other Forensic Adventures*, Toronto: McClelland & Stewart.
3. Maylunas, A. (1996), *A Lifelong Passion: Nicholas and Alexandra – Their Own Story*, London: Weidenfeld & Nicolson.

Chapter 6: The secondary crime scene

1. James, S. and Eckert, W. (1999), *Interpretation of Bloodstain Evidence at Crime Scenes*, 2nd ed., Boca Raton, FL: CRC Press.

Chapter 7: The tertiary crime scene

1. *Baltic Pilot, vol. III: Gulf of Finland, Gulf of Bothnia and Aaland Islands*, 9th ed. (2003), Taunton: United Kingdom Hydrographic Office.
2. Pounder, D. (1992), 'Lecture Notes: Bodies from Water', Dundee: Department of Forensic Medicine, University of Dundee, http://www.dundee.ac.uk/forensicmedicine/notes/water.pdf. Accessed 30 March 2010.
3. See Pounder, D. (1995), 'Lecture Notes: Time of Death', Dundee: Department of Forensic Medicine, University of Dundee, http://www.dundee.ac.uk/forensicmedicine/notes/timedeath.pdf. Accessed 30 March 2010.
4. *Nicholas and Alexandra: The Last Imperial Family of Tsarist Russia – from the State Hermitage Museum and the State Archive of the Russian Federation* (1998), London: Booth-Clibborn Editions.

Chapter 8: Forensics prove the lie

1. The tutorial is available at http://library.med.utah.edu/WebPath/TUTORIAL/GUNS/GUNINTRO.html.
2. Cook, A. (2005), *To Kill Rasputin. The Life and Death of Grigori Rasputin*, Stroud: History Press.

Chapter 9: Dismantling the accepted version of events

1. GARF Rasputin file.
2. Vyrubova. A (1923), *Memories of the Russian Court*, London: Macmillan. Available on the Alexander Palace website.

Chapter 10: Who did and who didn't kill Rasputin

1. Shishkin, O. (2000), *Ubit' Rasputina*, Moscow: Olma-Press.
2. Cook, A. (2005), *To Kill Rasputin. The Life and Death of Grigori Rasputin*, Stroud: History Press.
3. Le Queux, W. (1918), *The Minister of Evil: The Secret History of Rasputin's Betrayal of Russia*, London: Cassell.
4. Moynahan, B. (1997), *Rasputin: The Saint Who Sinned*, New York: Random House.

INDEX